SHIVA

Plant Myths and Traditions in India.
From Daityas to Devatas in Hindu Mythology.
Loves of Hindu Gods and Sages.
Surya, the Sun-god.
Biography of Birbal Sahni.
Festivals, Fairs and Fasts of India.
Karttikeya, the Son of Shiva.
Vishnu and His Incarnations.

SHIVA

SHAKTI M. GUPTA

SOMAIYA PUBLICATION PVT. LTD.
BOMBAY NEW DELHI

© 1979 SHAKTI M. GUPTA
1993 SECOND REVISED EDITION

SOMAIYA PUBLICATIONS PVT. LTD.

Registered Office:

172, Mumbai Marathi Granthasangrahalaya Marg
Dadar, Bombay - 400014
Tel: 4130230

Branch

F-6, Bank of Baroda Building
Parliament Street
New Delhi - 110001
Tel: 3324939, 3324973

ISBN-81-7039-203-9

Published by T.V. Kunhi Krishnan for
SOMAIYA PUBLICATIONS PVT. LTD., Bombay-400014
and printed at Raj Press, New Delhi-110001.

FOR   ARUDRA

My first grand child

HINDU LUNAR MONTHS

Magha	:	January-February
Phalguna	:	February-March
Chaitra	:	March-April
Vaishakha	:	April-May
Jyestha	:	May-June
Ashadha	:	June-July
Shravana	:	July-August
Bhadra	:	August-September
Ashvin	:	September-October
Kartika	:	October-November
Agrahayana	:	November-December
Pausha	:	December-January

CONTENTS

The whole is all that
The whole is all this
The whole was born of the whole,
what remains is the whole.
- Ishavasya Upanishad

Some of the legends
given in this text
are of tribal origin

ACKNOWLEDGEMENT

The author is grateful to the Archaeological Survey of India for their permission to reproduce the photographs in this text:

LIST OF ILLUSTRATIONS

23. Head of Parvati, Ahichchatra
24. Arjuna approaching Shiva, Shiva-keshava Temple, Pushpagiri, Cuddapah.
25. Ganga, the wife of Shiva, Bihar, 8th cent. A.D.
26. Preta, companion of Shiva, Lingaraja Temple, Bhubaneshwar, 11th cent. A.D.
27. Shiva Bhairava, Ekapada Someshwara Temple, Mukhalingam, 10th-11th cent. A.D.
28. Shani, Rahu and Ketu, Navagraha Slab, Konarak, 13th cent. A.D.
29. Churning the Ocean of Milk, Mallikarjuna Temple, Pattadkal 7th cent. A.D.
30. Wives of the Seven Rishis, Tanjore Gallery
31. Shiva Somaskandamurti, Chidambaram, c. 12th cent. A.D.
32. Karttikeya, Indian Museum, Calcutta, 11th-12th cent. A.D.
33. Parashurama, Garhwa Fort, c. 9th cent. A.D.
34. Trimurti of Shiva, unprotected monument, Mukhalingam, 8th-9th cent. A.D.
35. Ravana shaking the Kailash Mountain, Virupaksha Temple, Pattadkal, 7th cent. A.D.
36. Shiva carrying the corpse of Sati, bronze piece in the Gwalior Museum.
37. Descent of the Ganges, Mahabalipuram, c. 700 A.D.
38. Gandharva and Apsara, the flying celestials, Badami, 7th cent. A.D.
39. Agni, the god of Fire, Mathura Museum, 8th cent. A.D.
40. A dwarf, a gana of Shiva, Allahabad Museum
41. Brahma, the Creator, Aihole, 7th cent. A.D.
42. Chaturmukha Linga, Indian Museum, Calcutta.
43. Shiva Ardhanarishvara, Gangaikondacholapuram, c. 11th cent. A.D.
44. Durga ready to kill evil, from Bhitari in Lucknow Museum, 8th cent. A.D.
45. Sapta-matrikas from Nalanda, Lucknow Museum, c. 8th-9th cent. A.D.
46. Chamunda, Asutosh Museum, Calcutta, c. 10th cent. A.D.
47. Kali, the personification of death and destruction, a bronze sculpture, Gwalior Museum.

The section containing the above plates appears at the end of the book.

1

MANIFESTATIONS OF SHIVA

That which is Here also exists There,
This is equal to That and That
Is the model of This.

In Hindu mythology and symbolism, Vishnu, Shiva and
Shakti, the Mother Goddess, are visualised as both terrible
and benign, creative and destructive, ugly and handsome.
Shiva and Vishnu are considered equal in stature. They
represent the destroying and preserving aspect of the
Supreme Soul. Vishnu becomes Shiva when the periodic
dissolution of the universe occurs, and Shiva becomes Vishnu
when the universe has to be created all over again. Brahma
is considered a mere agent of the creative functions of the
Creator. He is Prajapati, the first-born.

Whereas Vishnu typifies qualities of *sattva,* the fairer
aspects of life, Shiva typifies qualities of *tamas,* the darker
aspects of life. When Shiva is the Supreme Lord of the
universe, there is death and destruction, for he kills all evil.
His ascetism negates all joy. But at the same time, he also
bestows wisdom and peace, and in this respect he is also a
creator and a preserver, just as Vishnu is a destroyer.

Shiva is conceived both in his unborn, invisible form, *Sthanu*
or *Linga* form, as well as in his anthropomorphic, aspect. He
is worshipped under various manifestations and his worshipper
invokes him by names which depict different aspects of him.
His multiple antagonistic functions are described as his
playful manifestations, i.e., his *lila-murties.* His main
functions are five: (1) Anugrahamurti, the beneficent aspect;
(2) Samharamurti, the destructive aspect; (3) Bhikshatanamurti,
the vagrant aspect; (4) Nrittamurti, the Lord of dancers; (5)
Maheshamurti, the Great Lord.

Among his titles, the well-known are: Chandrashekhara, (god with the moon in his hair), Nilakantha (blue-throated), Jatadhara (wearing matted hair), Jalamurti (whose form is water), Kapalamalin (wearer of a garland of skulls), Sthanu (immutable), Virupaksha (of misformed eyes), Vishwanatha (Lord of the universe), Bhutesha (lord of the elements), Aghora (non-fearful), Gangadhar (supporter of Ganga), Somaskanda (father of Skanda), Ardhanarishvara (lord who is half woman), Girisha or Sikhareshvara (lord of the peak), Vaidyanatha (lord of the physicians), Kalasamhara (destroyer of Time), Pashupati (lord of animals), Shankara (the beneficent), Shiva (the auspicious); Rudra (the howler), Mrityumjaya (the death-conquering deity), Keshin (with matted hair), Uma-Maheshvara (husband of Uma), and many others.

Shiva is mostly worshipped in the form of a stone called the *Shiva-linga* which represents the male creative energy of Shiva. It is called *Dhruva*, the fixed or the immovable fundamental form. Shiva is a god without form or attributes and his *linga* is the *nirguna* state of the Supreme Soul. According to the Shaivites, one is entitled to the worship of Shiva in the *linga* form only when one is spiritually very advanced and can realise that Shiva exists in all forms.

According to the *Skanda-purana*: "The *linga* is the sky and the earth is its altar." *Linga* is the source of creation and is also the end of everything, movable and immovable. The material world is only the manifestation of Shiva and it appears in many forms, such as space, air, fire, water, earth, mind, the sun and the moon. These eight elements are known as *Ashtamurtis* or the eight-form image of Shiva. It was created by taking the five material elements and the two vital airs, heat and cold. The eighth is Mind or Consciousness which is usually invisible and that is why in the *Ashtamurti* form of Shiva, usually only seven faces are shown and the eighth is imagined. The material manifestation of life depends on the intergrated constitution of these aspects or energies. The *Vedas* mention eight Vasus, the Puranas cite eight *murties* of Shiva and the religious cults of Shiva worship prescribe eight handfuls of flowers for

offering to the deity. According to the Gita, there are eight
forms of lower nature, i.e., the physical body, and the vital
airs, and mind are its two superimposed summits.
Iconographically, the *Ashtamurti* form of Shiva is also depicted
as a fabulous animal with eight feet: four are the normal feet
and the other four feet project towards the sky. Symbolically,
the eight forms of Shiva are the eight feet of this, his
Sharabha incarnation. The four visible feet are earthly or
material representing the earth, water, fire and air; and the
four feet facing the sky are considered to be celestial and
represent his aspects which are invisible.

The Shaivas believe in the grace of Shiva but at the same
time believe in the theory of *karma* and rebirth. Real
worship according to them consists in doing good to all living
creatures because they are but His own form.

Linga is a symbol of spirituality. It implies creativity
which is invisible and unmanifest. It is the arrow which
Shiva shot to destory the three cities of the *asuras*. In
symbolism it is the arrow which pierced the axial centre of
the Earth, the atmosphere and the space above in such a
way that the three became one. Just as Time is three fold,
i.e., past, present and future, but eternity is one, similarly,
the eternal aspects of Shiva remain undifferentiated, but in
nature it is manifest, in three forms, i.e., the sun, the moon
and the fire. The sun symbolises heat, the moon symbolises
cold and the fire is a combination of both. Fire is the central
energy; the sun and the moon represent heat and cold, light
and darkness, the introvert and extrovert forces that are
constantly operating against the central, stable and
immovable principle called *Sthanu*. Shiva as the arch-yogi called
Yogeshvara, is in eternal union with himself and thus becomes
Sthanu or of *linga* form.

In the Rudra-Shiva doctrine, the theory of monotheism
and the impersonal Brahman is blended. He is the cause
of creation, a god without a second, one who controls the
entire universe, protects all and on the day of dissolution,
withdraws all. He is the god, knowing whom one can be
free from all bondage.

Once the gods approached Rudra and asked him to
disclose his identity and learnt that Rudra alone was, is and

will be. He is identified with all *Vedic* gods like Brahma, Prajapati, Agni, Indra, Soma, Varuna, etc., as well as with deities like Ganesha, Skanda and Uma. Among his manifestations are the seven worlds, eight planets, Time and the elements.

ANTIQUITY OF SHIVA WORSHIP

Shiva worship is of very great antiquiy and extended from Central Asia to Kanya Kumari in India. But the worship of *Shiva linga* form became popular only since the Gupta period. It is since then that the belief in the *Lingam* representing the *nirguna* state of Shiva became more widely spread.

According to Marshall, the figure on the seals of Mohenjodaro, C.2500 B.C. is of Shiva as Pashupati, a *yogic* form considered to be an important aspect of Shiva. This figure from Mohenjodaro had three faces, two arms and is seated in a *yogic* posture with an elephant, a tiger, a rhinoceros and a buffalo on both its sides. Another seal found at Mohenjodaro shows the same deity seated in a *yogic* posture with image of two *naags*, i. e., half-serpent, half-human beings kneeling on either side of the deity in prayer. Similar other seals of a deity with the face of a man and the body of an animal like a bull or an elephant have also been discovered from the same site. These figures are believed to be the earliest prototypes of Shiva statues, particularly the ones where a trident and a bull are present along with the figure of a diety. Marshall considers some of the terracottas found in the Indus valley as symbols of a phallus. It is likely that during the pre-*Vedic* period, the god was worshipped in his phallic symbol as a god of creation.

Coins from the 2nd-3rd century B.C. have *Shiva-lingas* engraved on them. Shiva is also found carved in his human form, suggesting thereby that he was worshipped at that time not only in his immovable *Dhruva* form called a *linga* but also in his anthropomorphic form.

Rudra in pre-*Vedic* society was a deity of transcendent darkness, i.e., *tamas*, the embodiment of disintegration. His epithet Shiva, meaning the aspicious, later replaced his Vedic name Rudra. The quality of *tamas* or the tendency towards disintegration has as its basis the philosophy that what has a beginning must come to an end, all that is born must die and all that comes into existence must cease to exist. Therefore, the power of destruction is nearest to non-existence. This universal power of destruction is Shiva, the Lord of sleep, due to whom, all elements come forth alive, exist when created and dissolve ultimately.   Shiva is centrifugal inertia tending towards universal annihilation, disintegration and dispersion.   From destruction arises creation, followed again by destruction and thus the cycle of birth and death continues.   Silence and obscurity are the ultimate refuge of all seeking salvation and Shiva is that boundless void, a shapeless, indefinable quality beyond which there is only non-existence, and unfathomable abyss. He is death personified. He is Hara who destroys all indiscriminately.   He is death of deaths, i.e., eternal life.   Because sleep also in a way removes all pain and suffering, Rudra is called Shiva, the lord of sleep, a more peaceful aspect of Rudra.

According to the Upanishads: "Beyond this darkness, there is neither day nor night, neither existence nor non-existence but Shiva alone, the indestructible, and even the Sun lies prostrate before him."

In the *Rig-Veda*, god is referred as Rudra which means the Howler. According to a legend, when the life-principle became manifest, it cried as it had no name and Prajapati gave it the name Rudra. Rudra is associated with destructive phenomena like thunderstorms and epidemics. According to Bhandarkar, as time passed, the malignant Rudra, was transformed into the benign Shiva. Even though Rudra is conceived as a destructive force, he is also prayed for beneficent measures and is thus conceived as possessing two-fold characteristics, one fearful, the other desirable.   He is represented as Pashupati, the protector of cattle and children and at the same time possesses weapons which slay men and cows.   Out of his eight names, Rudra, Sarva, Ugra and Ashani or Bhima are the names of his destructive aspect, and Bhava, Pashupati, Mahadeva and Ishana of his beneficent nature. It was from this concept that the *Ashtamurti* of Shiva and of his son Kumara, developed.   Of these eight manifestations, each singly is incapable of creating life.   Only when they combine as one, life manifests. According to the doctrine of *Ashtamurti*, the eight manifestations represent: Sarva or Sadyojata (Prithivi or earth); Bhava or Vamadeva (Jala-murti;) Rudra or Aghora (Agni-murti); Ugra or Tatpurusha (Vayu-murti); Bhima or Ashani (Akasha-murti), Mahadeva or Apana (Chandra-murti); Ishana or Prana (Surya-murti); which also represents mind or consciousness; Pashupati (Yajna-murti).

RUDRA, THE LORD OF TEARS

Rudra, the Howler, appears in the *Vedas* as a powerful and dangerous god. The word Rudra means a remover of pain whether physical, mental or spiritual. He is the 'Great Fear' the thunderbolt, whom even the *devatas* feared. It is the anger of Rudra that is worshipped. It is the thunder in the sky, giving lightning which frightens men and at the same time brings rain which is necessary for an agricultural economy which was perhaps the original thought behind the worship of Rudra-Shiva. He is also the embodiment of sun, a form of the celestial fire which dries up life. His wife is called Suvarchala and their son is the planet Saturn.

Agni, the Lord of Fire, is considered as a manifestation of Rudra, for Agni's wrath destroys, and all that burns also pertains to Rudra. In his most destructive aspect, Rudra becomes Bhairava. Since Rudra is one of the solar divinities, he is called Bhuteshvara, the lord of elements. Later mythology made *bhuta* a ghost or a spirit and, therefore, Bhuteshvara became the god of spirits and ghosts. Rudra or Shiva as Bhuteshvara frequents cremation grounds, wears skulls and snakes and is attended upon by demons and imps.

SARVA (THE ARCHER)

Sarva represents the element earth (*Prithivi*) and, therefore, is considered as the Provider. He is also considered as the God of Love. His wife is Vikeshi or Dharani, the earth goddess, and their son is the planet Mars. As he is considered the son of the earth, i.e., *Bhumi*, he is called Bhauma.

UGRA (THE FEARFUL)

Ugra, the fearful, is also called Ashani the thunderbolt and is the spark that is responsible for final universal destruction. He is the devourer of offerings. His wife is called Diksha and their son is Santana or libation.

BHIMA OR ASHANI (THE TREMENDOUS)

Bhima is the embodiment of ether. He fulfils the desires of all beings. His wife is Disha, the directions of space and their son is Creation itself,called Sarga.

BHAVA (EXISTENCE)

It is the element water and is sometimes shown as an attendant of Shiva and is equated with Parjanya, the Lord of Rain. He is the all-powerful god whose consort is Uma and their son is the planet Venus.

PASHUPATI (THE HERDSMAN)

Pasupati is the embodiment of fire. Since he represents the element fire, he is the feeder of sacrifices and his wife is Svaha, the invocation at offerings and their son is *Skanda*, the god of war.

ISHANA (THE RULER)

He is the embodiment of air and a nourisher of all beings. His consort is called Shiva and their son is called *Manojana*.

MAHADEVA (THE GREAT GOD)

He is the reproductive power creating what is destroyed. He is the god with the phallus as his emblem. His seed is kept in the cup of the moon which is an embodiment of gentleness. His wife is Rohini and their son is the planet Mercury.

CREATION OF MARUTS, THE STORM-GODS

Rudra is considered as the creator of *Maruts*. He is as such called upon to avert cow-slaying, lightning, disease and pestilence. He is the kindly god who averts destruction and

death in every form. According to a legend, Indra, the king
of the celestials with his thunderbolt, dashed the unborn child
of Diti and Kashyapa into forty-nine pieces. Later, out of
compassion, he converted these lumps of flesh into Maruts
who became the storm-gods. Shiva and Parvati saw them
in great pain and Parvati asked Shiva to convert the lumps
of flesh into boys. Shiva made them into boys of like age
and appearance and presented them to Parvati. Parvati
adopted them and since then they are called sons of Shiva
and Parvati.

SHIVA-SHAKTI

Shiva who is free from illusion has neither a beginning
nor an end. He is in the form of pure knowledge. This form,
which is without a second, is light. He is the splendour,
the truth, the eternal bliss. This Being which has no form
of his own, wished to create an auspicious form, a part of
himself and yet endowed with all the powers, qualities and
knowledge of everything. He wished to create a form that
could go everywhere, see all, in fact, a Being of all forms,
a form that would be the cause of all, respected by all, the
beginning of all and one that would sanctify everything and
create everything. So he created a form of pure nature that
was called Ishvara. The manifest form of this formless Being
is known as *Sadashiva*.

This Being called Ishvara created a physical form of a
female who was called *Shakti*. This Shakti is called by
various names such as Pradhana, Prakriti, Maya, Gunavati,
Para, Ambika, Durga. She is the goddess of all, the Prime
Cause and the mother of the three deities. Eight-armed, this
Shakti radiates a splendour equalling a thousand moons and
stars. Her eyes shine like a full-blossomed lotus and she
is adorned with weapons and ornaments. She is the
generating cause of all and her brilliance cannot even be
conceived. She appeared as Maya, i.e., illusion, and gave
birth to the universe. As dormant energy, she is called
Kundalini and is depicted as a serpent who, on killing,
destroys the illusion of life and liberates the devotee from
the cycle of birth and death. When this *Kundalini Shakti*
coils round Shiva, the universe goes to sleep.

2

ICONOGRAPHY OF SHIVA

Shiva is usually depicted in his emblem of a phallus. When shown in an anthropomorphic form, he is mostly shown with his consort Uma, and seated on a bull that is white as the snowy peaks of the Himalayas and attended by men, serpents, *Gandharvas, Kinnaras* and elements of darkness such as the antigods, demons, imps, ghosts, spirits, animals, etc.

Even though Shiva is the embodiment of darkness, he is shown as white in colour because the two opposite tendencies, darkness and light, are inseparable. Darkness is surrounded by light and light is enveloped in darkness. White colour is the basic colour and all other colours are superimposed upon it. White exists before and remains after all other colours have disappeared. Therefore, white alone can be the colour of Shiva.

Shiva is three-eyed, wears the crescent moon as a diadem on his forehead and carries the celestial Ganga called Mandakini, an emblem of purity, in his matted hair. River Ganga represents the world of creation in its myriad forms and the matted hair of Shiva are complications in the affairs of the world. Ganga is the ceaseless flow from the beginning to the end of Time. Like Shiva, the colour of Ganga is also white. Shiva's body is smeared with ashes and he is ornamented with shining armlets. He wears a garland of pearls and snakes and has a tiger-skin for a loin cloth. Of his four hands, one carries the trident and the other an axe. One hand is in the gesture of granting boons and the other of removing fear. The four arms represent the four directions of space and are the signs of universal power.

The three eyes of Shiva represent the three lights: the sun, the moon, the fire, which illumine the earth, space and the sky. Through his eyes, Shiva can see the three forms of time: past, present and the future. His third eye, the frontal one, being the eye of higher perception, mainly looks inwards. When directed outwards, it burns all that appears before it. Because of his three eyes, he is known as *Trinetra, Tri-ambaka, Tri-aksha, Tri-nayana*. And because of the odd eye, as *Virupaksha*.

Shiva wears the crescent moon as a diadem on his forehead and is, called *Chandrashekhara*. Moon is the cup of ambrosia, also of offerings and the chalice of semen. He is considered as the power of sublimated Eros. According to a legend, Soma, the moon was discredited by the gods for eloping with Bhadra, the wife of Brihaspati, the preceptor of gods, and, as a punishment was cast into the ocean. Shiva honoured him by wearing him as a diadem when he arose out of the ocean when the latter was churned for ambrosia. He represents the principle of intelligence and consciousness.

The symbol of Shiva is the *trishula*, the trident which represents symbolically the three qualities of Shiva, i. e., the Supreme Soul as the Creator, the Preserver and the Destroyer. Another weapon of Shiva is the spear called *Pashupata*, a weapon with which he kills evil and at the end of the *yugas* destroys the entire universe. This spear is also called *Brahmashiras*. Shiva gave this spear to Arjuna, one of the Pandava princes of the Mahabharata fame. Arjuna propitiated Shiva for a long time, and ultimately pleased with his penance, Shiva appeared before Arjuna and granted him the spear so that Arjuna could vanquish his enemies, the Kurus.

Other weapons of Shiva include an axe called *Parashu* which Shiva gave to Parashurama to destroy the Kshatriyas. Shiva also carries a bow made of a serpent which has seven heads and poisonous teeth. The bow called *Pinaka* gives the epithet *Pinakin* to him. He also carries a club called *Khatvanga* which has a skull at its head. Sometimes he is shown holding an antelope in one of his hands at the back.

Shiva wears a garland of skulls and is thus called *Kapalin*. He carries a noose with which he binds offenders.

At the end of the universal destruction when all is a heap
of ashes, only Shiva remains.   Shiva, after this universal
destruction, smears himself with its ashes, *bhasma*.   It
signifies that fire is always accompanied by ashes, and
creation is conceived as the refuse that follows a universal
conflagration.   He also carries an hour-glass shaped drum
called *damaru* which heralds creation.

The vehicle of Shiva is a bull called *Vrishabha* or *Virsha*,
more popularly known as *Nandi*.   Symbolically, Nandi
represents the fecundating energy of Kamadeva, the god of
love, whom Shiva conquered.   And that is why Shiva is known
as *Nandikeshvara* (the lord of Nandi).   Nandi signifies love
and pleasure which are the source of all creation.   He is the
embodiment of justice and virtue and a mythical teacher of
dance and music.   Sometimes he is depicted as a man with
the head of a bull.

HOW THE WORSHIP OF SHIVA-LINGA STARTED

According to a story in the *Puranas*, Shiva and Vishnu
went to the Devadaruvana (a forest of *Cedrus deodara*) to
test the forbearance of hermits living in that forest.   Shiva
went stark naked and Vishnu was dressed as a beautiful
woman.   The sons of the hermits were captivated by the
beauty of the woman, i.e., Vishnu in disguise, and wherever
she went, they followed her with a burning desire. The daughters
and daughters-in-law of the *rishis* were likewise enchanted
by the grace and youth of Shiva.   They ran after him and
offered him their womanhood.   Shiva and Vishnu were
moving out of the forest with the young men and women
following them when the *rishis*, apprised of the situation,
came running and caught the mischievous pair.   Vishnu made
his escape in the tumult that followed.   But Shiva was badly
handled by the revengeful *rishis*.

The *rishis* first threw a poisonous snake at Shiva. The latter
caught the snake and wrapped it round his neck as a garland.
Next they threw an antelope at him which also he caught in his
hands. Symbolically, an antelope is the individual life or *prana*
which runs at the sight of the hunter but cannot escape him.
The   hunter   is   death   personified.   This   life-principle,
symbolised by the animal, is for sacrifice at the altar of
death, and Shiva is his only hope of salvation.

The *rishis* then sent a ferocious tiger to devour him. Shiva skinned the tiger and used its hide to wrap round himself. Next a demon in the form of an elephant was sent to trample him underfoot but Shiva skinned it also and covered himself with it. Thus was created the image of Shiva as *Gajasamhara*. And finally, the *rishis* mercilessly chopped off his organ of generation. And as soon as the divine phallus fell to the ground, it began to assume a stupendous size and pervaded the entire universe. Brahma and Vishnu entered the *Lingam* to find out its proportions but did not succeed.

Another version regarding the origin of the *Linga* form of Shiva is as follows: Vishnu in his anthropomorphic form was floating on the primeaval waters between the lifeless interval of dissolution and creation when he perceived another luminous being approaching him with great speed. This was the four-headed creator Brahma who enquired of Vishnu.

"Who are you? I am the first progenitor and create all. But how did you originate?"

Vishnu was annoyed at the audacity of Brahma and begged to differ from the claim he made. He said that he was the Creator and Destroyer of the universe. A quarrel arose between them, each contesting to be the Creator. They kept on arguing in the Timeless void under the starless sky when they saw rising out of the ocean a towering *Lingam* crowned with flames. The two divinities, Vishnu and Brahma, were so struck with amazement at this apparition that they forgot their quarrel. Brahma suggested that they find its height and its depth and offered to fly upwards into heaven while Vishnu dived into the depths of the ocean in search of the lower end of the *Lingam*. Vishnu took the form of a boar and entered the netherworld called *Patala*. He continued to go deeper into the ocean but the *Lingam* grew bigger and bigger and Vishnu could not find its lower end. Brahma met with a similar fate. Brahma in the form of a swan flew high into the heavens trying to find its upper limit. But the *Lingam* continued to grow bigger and Brahma could not reach its upper limit. They returned from their assigned errands and stood gazing with amazement at the evergrowing *Lingam*. Just then the side of the phallus burst

open and in its niche was standing Shiva who announced
to the two deities that he was their progenitor, the Supreme
Shiva who was the Creator, the Preserver and the Destroyer.
He said that Brahma was his right side and Vishnu his left
side and collectively they all existed in Shiva, the Supreme.
He afterwards formulated the law that he must be
worshipped in his phallic emblem and not in his
anthropomorphic form.

An addition to the above story says that when Brahma
and Vishnu returned after their futile attempt at finding the
height and the depth of the *Lingam*, Vishnu admitted his
defeat but Brahma told a lie and said that he had reached
the height of the *Lingam*. In defence he produced the Ketaki
flowers as witness. Shiva cursed the Ketaki plant (Pandanus
odoratissimus) for bearing false witness and said that its
flowers would never be offered in worship. Brahma was
cursed not to have his own temple or festival but, at the
request of Vishnu and other gods, he relented and said:

"In all domestic and public sacrifices you will be the
presiding deity. Even if a sacrifice is complete with all rites
and offerings, it will be fruitless without you."

A Vaishnava twist to the legend which gives the reason
for Shiva to be worshipped only in his phallic emblem is as
follows:

Once the seven celestial *rishis* got together to decide
which of the three gods, Brahma, Vishnu, Shiva, deserved
their worship. Since even after prolonged discussions, they
could not come to any decision, they asked *rishi* Bhrigu to
find out the merits of each god, so that the one most deserving
could be worshipped by them as the Supreme God.

Bhrigu first went to visit Brahma. Brahma was sitting
surrounded by his admirers and enveloped in his own
greatness. Being the custodian of the *Vedas*, i.e., knowledge,
he was proud and arrogant and considered all others beneath
him. When Bhrigu visited him, Brahma did not show him
the customary respect due to a Brahmana and Bhrigu cursed
him never to be worshipped.

Till today, even though Brahma is included in all
worship, he is never worshipped alone and no temple is
erected solely for his worship.

Next Bhrigu visited Shiva. Shiva was engaged in an amorous dalliance with his wife. Bhrigu, after waiting for hundreds of years and failing to meet Shiva, went away in disgust after cursing him to be worshipped only in his phallic emblem as qualities of darkness were dear to him.

Finally, Bhrigu visited Vishnu. Vishnu was fast asleep on his serpent-couch floating on the primeaval waters. Bhrigu again waited for a long time and ultimately, getting impatient, kicked the sleeping god in the chest. He was sure that Vishnu would be incensed at his audacity and was prepared for a volley of abuse. But to his surprise, Vishnu opened his eyes and gently stroked his foot that had kicked him and enquired of Bhrigu if the foot had been hurt. Bhrigu was taken aback at the humility of the god and decided that he alone out of the trinity of gods deserved to be worshipped.

DIFFERENT TYPES OF SHIVALINGAS

According to the *Agni-purana*, the *Lingam* is made of different substances like common salt, clarified butter, a piece of cloth, clay, wood, stone, pearl, gold, iron, silver, copper, brass, zinc, mercury and, of many other substances.

There are twelve *Jyotir-lingas*. These are: (i) Somanatha, near Pattan in Gujarat; (ii) Mallikarjuna or Srisaila in Andhra Pradesh; (iii) Mahakala or Mahakaleshvara at Ujjain in Madhya Pradesh; (iv) Omkara in Mandhata on the river Narmada; (v) Nageshwara in the Darukavana; (vi) Vaidyanatha in the Beed district of Maharashtra; (vii) Rameshvara on an island on the south coast of India, Tamil Nadu; (viii) Bhima-Shankara in the Rajamundy district; (ix) Visveshvara at Kashi in Uttar Pradesh.; (x) Ghrishneshwar or Vamashvara (near Ellora); (xi) Kedarnatha in the Himalayas, Uttar Pradesh; (xii) Tryambaka on the banks of the river Gautami, Maharashtra.

A *Jyotirlinga* symbolises Shiva as a light or fire. Every *Jyotirlingas* appearance or installation has its own legend. A *linga* originally meant the form of the Supreme Soul Shiva as conceived by his devotees. This form is divided into the soul in the living body and as the endless body of the entire universe. The upper portion of the *linga* represents *Akash* (ether) and, the lower portion the earth.

As time passed, various types of *Shiva lingas* came into
existence. Broadly speaking, they are divided into the man-
made *lingas* and the original *lingas* found in nature. They
are also divided into movable (*chala*) and immovable (*achala*)
types. A large number of *lingas* are named after the nine planets
(the *Navagrahas)*, the *Saptarishis*, celestial and Vedic gods,
sacred rivers, cities and mountains. The *lingas* found in
nature have various kinds of markings on them by which
they are identified and categorised. A *linga* may resemble
a lotus fruit, a ring, a ripe berry, an egg of a hen or a
duck, or it may have the distinctive sign of a particular god.
The following signs represent the various gods: The sign of
an umbrella represents Indra; one with the upper portion
looking like a conch represents Vishnu; with a two-headed
mark is Agni; with an imprint of three feet is Yama, the
god of death; shaped like a sword is Nairrata; Varuna is
represented with a pitcher-shaped *linga*; with a flag-mast
is Vayu, the god of wind; Kubera's sign is a club; Ishana
has the sign of a trident and a Brahma *linga* has a lotus
carved at its tip.

The *asura* king Bana was a devotee of Shiva. He used to
prepare daily a fresh *linga* out of earth for worshipping Shiva.
Pleased with his devotion Shiva himself appeared before him and
offered him a boon. Banasura then said: "If you are pleased with
my devotion, then grant me a boon of a permanent *lingam* that
I can daily worship and do not have to prepare a fresh *lingam*
every day." As soon as the boon was granted by Shiva, 14 crore
lingas appeared all over the world for the devotees of Shiva to
worship. Since these *lingas* were created at the request of Bana,
they came to be called *Bana-lingas*. *Bana-linga* stands for
Sadashiva whose other name is Bana and it is a permanent symbol
of Shiva.

THE JYOTIRLINGAS

(1) SOMANATHA is situated in Saurashtra in Gujarat.
Soma also called Chandra, the personified moon married 27
daughters of Daksha but he was partial to Rohini among
them and the other wives complained to their father. Daksha
cursed his son-in-law Soma with the wasting disease
consumption. On Soma asking for forgiveness, the curse was

modified. Soma and his wife Rohini were asked by Daksha
to proceed to the western coast of Gujarat and perform
austerities and undergo penance which they did for 4000
years. Shiva pleased appeared before them and said that the
moon would shine for 15 days of the month and wane for
the next fifteen days, and thus he would not waste away
totally. As a thanks-giving, Soma established a *linga* there
named after him as Somanatha.

This area is also known as Prabhaskashetra, the area
of radiance as Soma regained his radiance there.

(2) MALLIKARJUNA is present on the sacred hill
Srisaila or Sriparvata along the banks of the river Krishna
in Andhra Pradesh. The story goes that a king of
Chandraguptapura fell in love with his daughter Chandravati.
She cursed him and he was drowned after which Chandravati
became an ascetic and started living among the cowherds.
She noticed that one of the cows always came back after
grazing without any milk in her udders. Presuming that
someone was milking her when she went out to graze,
Chandravati decided to investigate and found that the cow
discharged her full udders on a *linga*. (This story with slight
variations is associated with many Shiva temples). That
night Shiva appeared in a dream and told her that he was
residing in that *linga*. Chandravati built a temple over the
linga and worshipped it with flowers of Mallika (Jasminium
sambac). Because of the Mallika flowers offered in worship,
the *Jyotirlinga* came to be called Mallikarjuna. It grants
whatever the devotee desires.

(3) MAHAKALESHVARA: In Madhya Pradesh on the
banks of the river Kshipara, in the town of Ujjain is present
the *Jyotirlinga* called Mahakaleshvara. Both Vishnu and
Shiva met here in mutual adoration and worship, offering
Tulasi leaves (Ocimum sanctum) and Bilva leaves (Aegle
marmelos). A few kilometers outside Ujjain in the *ashrama*
of Krishna's guru Sandipani lived a devout Brahmana called
Vedapriya under whom the city flourished and came to be
known for its prosperity. A *rakshasa* called Dushana
attracted by its prosperity, came along with his army to
conquer the city. Since the Brahmanas did not possess an

army to protect their city, they prayed to Shiva at the
Jyotirlinga. When Dushana came to attack them, the earth
caved in and from the pit thus formed, appeared Shiva as
Mahakala, and the *rakshasas* were all reduced to ashes. Since
then   the *Jyotirlinga* at Ujjain came to be known as
Mahakaleshvara.

(4) OMKARESHVARA *Jyotirlinga* is present on an
island shaped like the sacred syllable OM (AUM) in the river
Narmada, thus giving this *Jyotirlinga* its name. According
to a legend, *rishi* Narada made fun of the Vindhya mountains
here comparing them with Mt.Meru and said that they could
never compete with Mt.Meru who was greater in stature and
divinity. Vindhya was distressed and decided to propitiate
Shiva, the lord of the universe. He went to Omkara made
an earthern *linga* and worshipped him. Shiva was pleased
and agreed to stay there. Mandhata, a king of the solar
dynasty, performed a hundred *Yajnas* here and the divinity
is said to be present in a natural spring which is held sacred.
The *Jyotirlinga* here is worshipped with 30,000 earthern
lamps which are made daily afresh by 22 worshipers. Shiva
resides in the syllable Omkara as well as the earthern *lingas*
at Omkara Mandhata.

(5) KEDARESHVARA: is present in the Himalayas,
in the Tehri Garhwal region of Uttar Pradesh. The Pandavas
worshipped Shiva at Varanasi to atone for the sin of killing
their kin. To test their devotion to him, Shiva left Varanasi
(Kashi) and went to the Himalayas. The Pandavas tracked
him there but he disappeared at Gupta Kashi (hidden Kashi)
and re-appeared among the herd of cattle as a bull. Bhima,
the second Pandava brother spotted him and waited for the
herd of cattle to come home. Bhima tried to catch him but
Shiva as a bull again managed to slip but Bhima kept on
holding his rump which pleased Shiva immensely and he
decided to stay back as a *Linga*. The Kedareshvara
Jyotirlinga is shaped as the rump of a bull. It is the
northernmost *Jyotirlinga*. Pandavas on their last journey
went up the Himalayas this way. Adi Shankarcharya also
followed the same route and never returned. It was at the
request of the two fold incarnations of Vishnu as Nara and

Narayana that Shiva stayed in Kedara on the mountain Himavat, and was worshipped by them daily.

(6) BHIMA SHANKARA: This *Jyotirlinga* is situated in the Sahyadri range, in Maharashtra, an area which has many legends regarding this *linga*. It is named after Bhima, the son of Kumbhakarna and Karkati. Karkati was molested by Kumbhakarna, the brother of Ravana and discarded by her husband. Bhima, Kumbhakarna and Ravana were devotees of Shiva. They were all killed by Ramachandra in his fight with Ravana to rescue Sita. Bhima had acquired great powers and when he was about to kill a Shiva devotee by breaking the clay *linga* that he worshipped, Shiva took his terrifying form as Bhimeshvara and appeared before him. A fierce battle was fought between them. Narada requested Shiva not to waste his time and kill him by a mere sound *Humkara*, and he was killed accordingly.

Another legend mentions that the name Bhimashankara is because of the huge rock in the shape of Bhima on which Shiva rested after killing the Tripurasuras and the sweat from his body trickled down and formed the river Bhima on the banks of which is this *Jyotirlinga*.

(7) KASHI VISHVESHVARA Jyotirlinga is at Varanasi, present in the form of a cosmic egg, and bestows worldly pleasures and salvations. He is worshipped by Vishnu and other gods as well as by Kubera and Bhairava.The Himalaya mountains are the abode of Parvati's parents, Mena and Parvata. Shiva and Parvati after their marriage lived on Mt. kailash, also in the Himalayas. After being married for a while, Parvati felt that they should not reside in the Himalayas and chose Varanasi (Kashi) as an alternative abode. Kashi was the Capital of king Divodasa and he being very fond of his city, did not wish to leave it. Vishnu so arranged that Divodasa lost all interest in worldly matters and possessions and left Kashi on his own. After that Shiva himself installed the *Linga* which came to be famous by the name of Kashi Visveshara. Varanasi is a strong *shaivite* hold and it is here that Adi Shankarcharya preached his advaita doctrine. Parvati is worshipped as Annapurna here, the provider of food and she never ate before her devotees had eaten.

The *Lingam* installed at Kashi is also called Kandeshvara.
It is supposed to be the ball of Parvati which changed into
this phallic image after hitting the demons, Vidala and
Utpala .This image of the *Linga* destroys the wicked but
is favourably disposed towards its devotees whom it grants
worldly pleasures and salvation.

(8) TRYMBAKESHVARA is present in Maharashtra
20 miles from Nasik, on the Brahmagiri mountains on the
banks of the Godavari, also known as Gautami as *rishi*
Gautam had his *ashrama* on its banks. During a severe
drought, *rishis* with their families stayed at this *ashrama*
and were well looked after by ,*rishi* Gautam. The wives
of the *rishis* instead of feeling greatful, felt slighted on
having to wait till the disciples of Gautam drew water for
him and conveyed their resentment to their husbands. When
the draught was over, the *rishis* with their families decided
to leave but *rishi* Gautam wished them to stay on. *Rishis*
did not want to annoy him and planned a ruse by which
they could leave. They made Ganesha appear as a weak
cow grazing near the *ashrama* . When Gautam tried to drive
it away, it fell down dead. To atone for the sin of cow-
slaughter, he prayed to river Ganga to come to him but
Ganga refused. To change her course, Shiva hid his tresses
in Brahmagiri which forced Ganga to flow as *Go-dana,* i.e.
gift of life to the cow. And thus the river came to be called
Godavari.

(9) VAIDYANATHA *Jyotirlinga* is present in the
Beed district of Marathawada in Maharashtra and is known
there as Parli-Vaidyanatha. This *Jyotirlinga* symbolises good
health and long life and is associated with rishi Markandeya
who was saved from death by Shiva. Vaidyanath is the
celestial physician. Harihara, the united form of Vishnu and
Shiva, as well as Dhanwantri, the founder of Ayurveda
system of medicine, entered this *linga.*

According to a legend, Ravana had 10 heads, nine
of which he cut off doing severe penance but they were
restored each time by Shiva as Vaidyanatha. Shiva pleased
with his devotion, presented Ravana with a *linga* as a reward
but warned him that if he put it down anywhere, it would

remain rooted there. Ravana carrying the *linga* on his way
to Lanka, gave it to a cowherd while he himself went to
relieve himself. Since Ravana took a long time to return,
the cowherd got tired holding it and put it down and went
away. Since then it has remained rooted in Marathawada.
In order to fetch Shiva to earth, he was installed as a
Jyotirlinga in the cremation grounds.

(10) NAGANATHA, NAGESHVARA *Jyotirlinga* is
situated at Oundh, east of Ahmedanagar in Maharashtra in
the Darukavana. *Asuras* had earlier been granted a boon
by Shiva for their penance and worship of him. But they
soon started harassing the *devatas*. Ogress Daruka and her
husband were given an area where the *devatas* were
forbidden to enter to save them from harassment. The *asuras*
started propitiating Shiva and recited the sacred *mantra* OM
NAMAH SHIVAYA. The resonance was so great that it
reached Mt. Kailash and disturbed Shiva and he came down
from his mountain retreat to kill the *asuras*. Since at that
time, Shiva had *naags* all over him, he came to be called
Naganatha, the lord of snakes and Nageshvara, the god of
snakes. Shiva's wife Parvati became Nageshvari and both
of them reside in this *Jyotirlinga*. Shiva manifested himself
as the destroyer of the wicked. He killed *rakshasa* Daruka,
a violator of virtue and saved his devotee Supriya who was
a merchant.

(11) RAMESHVARAM: *Jyotirlinga* is present in
Tamil Nadu on the banks of the ocean and is named after
Ramachandra, the seventh incarnation of Vishnu, who
installed it. Rama was very upset at the time of war with
Ravana which resulted in a great loss of life. The *rishis*
advised him to install a *linga* and worship it. Rama asked
Hanuman to bring one from Mt. Kailash. Since the auspicious
moment for the installation of the *linga* was drawing near
and Hanuman had not returned, Sita was asked by Rama
to make a *linga* of sand, which was installed by Rama. Just
then Hanuman arrived and wanted that the *linga* he had
brought should be installed instead. Rama asked him to
remove the *linga* already installed, but Hanuman could not
even shift that *linga* and fainted with the effort. The *linga*

had the power of Rama and Sita. To please Hanuman who had at his instigation brought a *linga* from Mt. Kailash, Rama installed it also and it is called Hanumandeshvara.

(12) GHUSHMESHVARA, GHRISHNESHVARA: is near Ellora in Maharashtra. There are various legends regarding the *Jyotirlinga* here. According to one legend, a childless couple, Sudharma and his wife Sudeha lived there. Sudeha persuaded her husband to marry her sister Ghushma so that she could bear a child. Ghushma's son grew up to be a handsome young man which roused Sudeha's jealousy and one day, she killed him and threw him into a lake. Ghushma used to immerse her clay *linga* in that lake called Shivalaya after worship and when she came near that lake, Shiva appeared and after narrating the gruesome deed, offered to kill Sudeha. But Ghushma did not wish to take a revenge and instead requested Shiva to stay there for ever. All the same, Shiva did revive her son and stayed there in his *linga* named after Ghushma. It is called Ghushmeshvara.

Another legend gives the name Ghrishneshvara to the *Jyotirlinga*. After her morning toilet, Parvati with her right thumb rubbed saffron on her left palm to make a *bindi* for applying on her forehead. As she was rubbing *(gharshana)* the saffron, a *linga* appeared from it and it was named Ghrishneshvara.

SHIVA MARRIES SATI

Long ago when evil forces ruled the universe, law and order was disrupted and utter chaos prevailed. Vishnu and Brahma, accompanied by their wives, visited Shiva and requested him to marry and produce progeny for the good of the world. Shiva agreed and asked if there was a woman who might suit his nature. Brahma named Sati who was really Shiva, the female energy of Shiva himself, born as a daughter of *rishi* Daksha. Daksha was the son of Aditi, the mother of gods. Aditi had earlier asked her first seven sons to create but, being immortal, they could not. Ultimately Daksha (also Martanda in some stories) agreed to create. He, being born a dead egg, represented death. Symbolically it means that for creation to succeed, the

polarity manifested by life and death has to be there. Aditi
represents immortality and Daksha represents the limiting
principle which is subject to destruction.

Kamadeva, the god of love, overheard the conversation
between Shiva and the gods who were arguing with him to
marry and finding that Shiva was at last willing to take
a wife, waited for an opportune moment to strike his arrows
of love at him. When Sati performed the *Nanda-vrata*, Shiva
appeared before Sati and under the influence of Kamadeva's
arrows, Harshana and Mohana, he granted her a boon and
promised that she would become his wife. Sati asked Shiva
to make the proposal of marriage to her father, as was
customary.

Shiva repaired to his abode on the Himalayas but, being
anxious to marry Sati, was restless and decided to sent
Brahma to arrange his marriage to Sati. Brahma went to
Daksha, got his consent to the marriage and in the presence
of sages like Narada, Marichi, etc., Daksha gave his daughter
in marriage to Shiva. After the marriage rites had been
performed, Vishnu arrived and asked Shiva to kill those who
looked passionately at Sati. Brahma, while performing the
marriage ceremony, became enamoured of Sati and his seed
fell on the ground. Shiva got enraged at him and was about
to kill him with his trident. The *rishis* present tried to
appease Shiva but the latter was adament on killing Brahma.
Vishnu pacified him by pointing out that all three of them,
i.e., Brahma, Vishnu and Shiva, were identical and part of
one another. Shiva was pacified by this explanation and
went away with Sati to Mr. Kailash.

Sati was happily married to Shiva but her father Daksha
was unhappy at her choice of husband. He called Shiva
by various names such as a beggar, a frequenter of cremation
grounds, a friend of goblins and imps.

Daksha performed a great sacrifice to which all great
and small divinities were invited but Shiva was left out as
he considered him unworthy of being invited to such an
august gathering. When Sati heard of the sacrifice, she was
incensed at the insult shown to her husband. She insisted
on Shiva going to the sacrifice and demanding his right as
a son-in-law. Shiva was at first reluctant to go but on Sati's

insistence, he agreed. He went to Daksha's sacrifice with Sati and created havoc. A fierce battle took place between Shiva's *ganas* and the gods and sages who had come to attend the sacrifice. Shiva's anger issued from his third eye. It took the form of a terrifying looking creature called Virabhadra and he destroyed Daksha's sacrifice. Many were killed or maimed; blood flowed like streams; the sacrificial offerings were scattered. Pushan grinned at Shiva and had his teeth pulled out. Bhaga was seized by Nandi and his eyes were pulled out by Virabhadra as he had made a sign with his eyes and thus insulted Shiva. Another legend regarding Bhaga's blindness says that Shiva-Rudra fought Prajapati as the latter wanted to commit incest with his daughter. The semen dropped by Prajapati was collected and offered as an oblation. Bhaga was standing towards the south end of the altar. He saw the semen and because of its brilliance, became blind. Bhaga means the sharer and he is considered blind because he makes no difference between great and small, the rich and the poor. In this respect, Bhaga is considered to be an aspect of Shiva and Shiva is called *Bhaganetrata*.

Towards the end of the battle, Daksha was beheaded. Sati seeing her father killed was upset and asked Shiva to revive him. Shiva agreed, but Daksha's head could not be found. So a goat was sacrificed and Daksha's head was replaced with that of the goat's. Daksha asked Shiva for forgiveness but in spite of that Sati, as a protest, committed *sati*. Shiva was inconsolable at the loss of his wife. He picked up Sati's charred body and roamed around the universe, lamenting her loss. Many years passed and slowly, Sati's body started disintegrating and fell off limb by limb. Wherever a part of Sati's body fell, that place became a centre of pilgrimage. There are 108 *Shakti pithas* of Sati.

The sacrifice or *yajna* performed in this legend is considered to be a lower kind of a sacrifice which is actually carried on in the human body through sensuous pleasures in which the higher mind is pulled down by an uncontrolled ego. Daksha's egoistic head was decapitated and replaced by the head of a goat. In Vedic symbolism, the goat called, Aja, is the unborn, universal Principle. It is only when a normal link is restored between the individual and the spiritual aspects of the soul, that an integrated form of human personality develops.

Daksha represents the individual ego *ahamkara*. Being a personification of Ego, he thought that he could function by himself and that the Universal energy of Aditi was not essential. His daughter Sati is an incarnation of Aditi whose presence for the performance of individual sacrifice is essential. With Sati dropping dead on the altar of sacrifice, the *yajna* automatically came to an end because without the universal creative energy as Sati or Shiva, no sacrifice could be complete. The Ego personified as Daksha made the grave mistake of not inviting them, and lost his head in the turmoil. The head is a symbol of mind and life. His head was replaced by that of a goat, which, as already pointed out, is the unknown universal Principle.

BIRTH OF MARS

After Sati's body completely disintegrated, Shiva returned to Mt. Kailash but there he felt her loss even more. In search of peace, he once again roamed all over the world, but not finding consolation anywhere, he returned to his mountain abode. Ultimately, he went into a trance. It was then that he found his imperishable real form. Thus Shiva remained for a long time, unaffected by anything and in a state of supreme bliss. When he came out of the trance, drops of sweat caused by exhaustion appeared on his forehead. The drops fell on earth and collectively took the shape of a child. The child had handsome features, was copper-coloured and four-armed. His brilliance was unbearable but he cried like a mortal child. Shiva was pre-occupied and the Earth, afraid that he might be disturbed by the crying of the child, took the guise of a woman and nursed him. In the absence of Sati, the Earth acted as his mother. Pleased with her, Shiva addressed her thus:

"O Earth, I bless you. Rear affectionately this child born of the glittering drops of my sweat. Although he is born of me, he will be famous by your name. He will be a bestower of pleasures on his devotees and will be endowed with good qualities. Accept him as your child."

As soon as Shiva had asked the Earth to adopt his son, he felt a great relief from the pangs of separation at his loss of Sati. The Earth was happy to have adopted Shiva's son and she returned to her abode with the child.

Since the earth is called *Bhumi*, the child acquired the name *Bhauma*, the son of the Earth. He attained youth immediately and worshipped Shiva and by his grace acquired the status of a planet. He is the planet Mars.

MENA AND OTHERS INCUR THE WRATH OF SANAKA

Brahma's son Daksha had sixty daughters all of whom in turn created various forms of life. They were married to Kashyapa and other holy sages. Among them Svadha was given to the fore-fathers. She had three virtuous daughters called Mena, Dhanya and Kalavati. They were mentally conceived daughters and not born of the womb of Svadha and were only conventionally considered as her daughters.

Once the three sisters went to Svetadvipa. About the same time, Siddhas, sons of Brahma, Sanaka and other celestial beings came there. On seeing them, the assembled people stood in reverence and bowed to them. But the three sisters were so surprised to see them that they just stared at them without making their obeisance.

On seeing such odd behaviour, Sanaka and others, unable to bear such insolent behaviour, admonished them: "In spite of being the daughters of the fore-fathers, you are foolish, bereft of wisdom and ignorant of the essence of the *Vedas*. You behave like mortals and do not pay us the customary respect. Therefore, we curse you to be born as mortal women."

The three sisters were greatly upset at the curse and begged forgiveness. But since a curse once pronounced could not be entirely removed, Sanatkumara modified it and said:

"Mena the eldest amongst you, shall become the wife of Himavat, the Mountain that is a part of Vishnu, and Parvati will be born as her daughter. The second sister Dhanya shall be the *yogini* wife of Janaka. Her daughter shall be Mahalakshmi named Sita. The youngest sister

Kalavati shall be the wife of *Vaishya* Vrishabhana. At the end of the *Dvapara-yuga*. Radha will be born to her."

And then he added: "Mena's daughter Parvati, after performing severe penance shall become the wife of Shiva and Mena and her husband Himavat shall attain the region of Mt. Kailash. Dhanya's daughter Sita shall become the wife of Ramachandra, who will be an incarnation of Vishnu and her father Janaka will be a living liberated soul and a great *yogi*. He will attain Vaikuntha. Kalavati's daughter Radha shall become the mistress of Krishna and shall be united with him in secret love. All three will be living as liberated souls and attain Gokula."

Mena married Himavat and in due course had a daughter whom the fond parents named *Parvati* as she was born of Parvata, the mountain. She is also called Girija for the same reason, Giri meaning a mountain. She is also called Aparna as she and her two sisters Ekaparna and Ekapatala propitiated Shiva to win him as a husband but while her two sisters subsisted on one leaf, Aparna subsisted on nothing. Her mother was worried for her life and cried in distress: "U-ma" which means 'O don't !' Since that time she came to be called Uma. Parvati or Uma went without food or rest for years on end and stood in ice-cold waters for long stretches of time till Shiva was satisfied with her penance and offered to marry her. Coming to know of Shiva's decision, *Kinnaras*, the half-animal, half-human beings, talked scandal and said:

"How can Shiva marry Parvati? We had ourselves overheard him giving his solemn word to Sati that he would not marry any other woman. If now he marries Parvati, it will be a breach of faith."

Vishnu and Brahma overheard this talk and replied: "Parvati is really Sati reincarnate and, therefore, by marrying her, Shiva would not really be going against his promise to Sati."

3

SHIVA MARRIES PARVATI

Marriage of Shiva and Parvati was solemnised with all attendant rituals. Gods, goddesses and *rishis* from all over the universe were present to grace the occasion. *Gandharvas* sang auspicious songs and the *apsaras* danced. The heavens showered celestial flowers on the couple, the earth turned green and brought forth abundant flowers and fruits and the rivers flowed merrily, watering the country-side. The only event to mar the festivities was the destruction of Kamadeva, the god of love. This happened shortly before the marriage of Shiva and Parvati took place.

KAMADEVA IS REDUCED TO ASHES

Before Shiva married Parvati, a powerful demon called Taraka was afflicting the deities, men and *rishis*. A time came when his atrocities became unbearable but the deities could not kill Taraka as he had a boon that he would meet his death only at the hands of a son of Shiva. But Shiva was for ever engrossed in his meditations and had no thought of getting married. When gods, men and *rishis* approached Vishnu, Brahma, Indra and other deities, a council was called and it was decided that Shiva should be persuaded to get married. For this, Vishnu's Yogamaya was considered the right choice of a wife for Shiva. It was decided that she should be born as Parvati, the daughter of Mena and Himavat, as Himavat is a part of Vishnu. It was arranged that while Parvati would practise austerities to win Shiva as her husband, Kamadeva, the god of love would go and incite amorous thoughts in Shiva.

One day while Shiva, the Mahayogi, was as usual deep

in meditation, Kamadeva with his friend Vasant, i. e., Spring, approached him. It was winter and the whole mountain range of Kailash was covered with snow. Cold, chilly winds blew day and night and the sky was always overcast. But as Vasanta approached Mt. Kailash where Shiva was in deep meditation, spring came. The sky turned azure blue, trees and bushes brought forth buds and flowers, bees flitted from flower to flower sucking honey and the birds chirped. The snows started melting and the rivers and streams overflowed their banks. Shiva opened his eyes and was surprised to find that spring had come out of season. Parvati was deep in meditation, propitiating him. Kamadeva was waiting for this moment. Finding his opportunity, he aimed his arrows of love at Shiva. Shiva immediately fell in love with Parvati and desired her. This was contrary to his normal nature and it surprised even him. Just then he saw Kamadeva with his bow and arrow and realised that he was the culprit. This infuriated him and he looked at Kamadeva in anger and the latter was reduced to ashes with the fire issuing from Shiva's third eye.

The image of Shiva as the destroyer of Kamadeva, is called *Kamantakamurti*. The killing of Kamadeva is an act of extreme renunciation. Only an arch-yogi like Shiva could overcome temptation and pleasures of the senses. Kamadeva is the great disturber of *yoga* as he has the power over sex. If Shiva had to complete his *samadhi*, which is limitless in time and space, it was absolutely essential for him to sublimate his instinct of love and that he did by burning Kamadeva to ashes. Shiva as the *Maha-yogi* is Agni or the mysterious vital Fire manifest in all matter. This fire consumed the god of love but re-created him in the subconscious world of the human mind as well as in the conscious spheres of the human body.

When Kamadeva was thus reduced to ashes, his wife Rati, i.e., Desire personified, lamented his death and begged Shiva to revive him. Shiva gave her a boon that Kamadeva would be reborn as a grandson of Krishna. But he also said that in future the god of love would not have any form. He would only exist as a power without form. But in spite of Shiva's resentment at Kamadeva inciting amorous thoughts in him for Parvati, he married her.

The metabolic energy called *Kundalini* is symbolised as Parvati. She is conceived as the Serpent Power which lies coiled in the lowest chambers of the human body. *Kundalini* when properly quickened unfolds her vibrating hoods and by an upward sweep enters the five plexi or centres within the spinal cord and then finally into the brain through what is called the *Krauncha-dvara* or magnum foremen. In mythology, Shiva's wedding with Parvati is the entrance of this Serpent Power into the Higher Mind which is compared to the snowy mountains of Kailash. Kailash is the symbol of the highest mind and Shiva has his abode on this mountain where silence reigns eternally. The simile is with a human wedding which releases the highest ecstasies of the flesh to the wedding of *Kundalini* with Shiva which is a symbol of the highest bliss attained by an individual soul.

This *Kundalini* or Serpent Power called Parvati was so beautiful that in the three worlds no one could compete with her. This gave her the epithet *Tripura-sundari*. Because of her beauty, many demons, *yakshas* and deities fell in love with her. Even Kubera, the god of wealth , saw her on the Himalayas while he was doing penance, and looked at her amorously. As a consequence, he lost one eye and had to do penance for a further period of five hundred years before Shiva forgave him.

In the Tantric cult, Parvati is identified with *Prakriti* itself and her three attributes *rajas, sattva* and *tamas* are the three gods Brahma, Vishnu and Shiva, respectively. Later Parvati came to be called by various names such as *Kali, Chandika, Chamunda, Vijaya, Jaya, Jayanti, Bhadrakali, Durga, Bhagavati, Kamakhya, Kamanda, Amba, Mridani, Sarvamangala, Ambika* and by many other names.

STORY OF THE SUBMARINE FIRE

After Shiva had reduced Kamadeva to ashes, the fire arising out of his third eye began to blaze uncontrolled and rapidly spread all over. Frightened at the approaching flames, deities took refuge with Brahma and requested him to save the universe. The fire was blazing brilliantly, ready to consume everything when Brahma, by the grace of Shiva, subdued it and made it into a tender flame which had the appearance of a mare and took it to the sea shore. The ocean took a human form and asked Brahma the reason for his visit.

Brahma answered: "This fire with the form of a mare is the fire of Shiva's wrath after it had killed Kamadeva. At Shiva's behest, I have suppressed it into this form and brought it to you. Be merciful to it and bear this fire till the final dissolution of the universe. His diet will be your waters. Don't let it go down. You must preserve it till I come for it."

The ocean agreed to take care of the fire which arose out of Shiva's fury at Kamadeva's audacity. The fire in the form of a mare entered the ocean and began to consume currents of water and blazed out of the ocean with shooting flames. The points from where the flames emerged out of the ocean came to be called *Badavamukha.*, (Jwalamukhi).

Though Brahma was part of Shiva and was always ready to do his bidding, yet at times his behaviour annoyed Shiva. For instance, when, *Sandhya*, i.e., twilight, personified as Brahma's daughter was born, Brahma got enamoured of her and attempted to seduce her. Sandhya got frightened and to escape him, turned into a deer. Brahma pursued her through the sky in the form of a stag. Shiva, who witnessed this, was annoyed at Brahma and shot an arrow at the stag. The arrow cut off the stag's head which remains in the sky in the 4th mansion called *mrigashirras* and the arrow in the 6th lunar mansion called *Ardha*. Sandhya is the wife of Shiva and is worshipped as a year-old baby.

BIRTH OF SKANDA

The *devatas* were worried at Shiva's dalliance with Parvati which extended over thousands of years but produced no result. They wanted Shiva's son to be born who was destined to kill the *asura*, Taraka. With this in mind, the *devatas* along with Brahma and Vishnu visited *Shivaloka* and eulogised Shiva who was with Parvati at the time, but

Shiva did not notice them. Having failed to attract the attention of Shiva, they decided that Agni, the god of fire, should be asked to approach Shiva and by his heat make him leave Parvati so that the *devatas* could place their petition before him. Agni was afraid of Shiva's curse as he remembered the fate of Kamadeva but afraid of the *devatas*, he agreed. He approached Shiva and by his powers generated so much heat that Shiva felt uncomfortable. He left Parvati's bed and asked the deities what their wish was. The deities asked him to produce a son who would slay Tarakasura. Shiva agreed and addressing the gathering, said: "whoever wishes to, can take this discharged semen of mine." Saying this, he let his semen fall on the ground. Urged by the gods, Agni became a dove and swallowed the semen with his beak. In the meantime, since Shiva took a long time to return, Parvati hastened to where Shiva was. On finding what had happened, she was furious and said to Vishnu and other gods who were present:

"You are wicked and selfish. For the sake of realising your selfish interests, you propitiated my husband and spoilt my dalliance with him. And because of that I have become a barren woman. After offending me, no one can be happy. Therefore, you wicked heaven-dwellers, you will always remain unhappy and dissatisfied. I curse the wives of the *devatas* to remain barren."

Prithvi (Earth) in turn cursed Parvati that she would never carry a child of Shiva in her womb and that explains why Parvati's two sons, Karttikeya and Ganesha have unusual births. Parvati by her curse banished the gods to earth and they turned into stone. This resulted in the gods being worshipped as stone images.

Blazing with fury, Parvati addressed Agni and said: "You have carried out the task of the gods. You are a fool, a rogue and a wretched vile person who pays heed to the counsel of the wicked. It was neither proper nor wise of you to have swallowed Shiva's semen. You are ignorant of Shiva's fundamental principles. I curse you to be the devourer of everything." After thus cursing the gods, Parvati returned to Shiva's apartments.

According to the *Vedic* texts, gods partake of the offerings of food consigned to the fire. Shiva's semen having been swallowed by Agni, the god of fire, the gods became pregnant. But unable to endure the force of the semen, they were scorched and afflicted by the heat produced by it. In desperation, they approached Shiva and said, "O Shiva, we admit that your power is incapable of being transgressed. We have become pregnant and also scorched by your semen. Please take pity on us and remove our plight."

Shiva took pity on the gods and suggested to them to vomit his semen virile. Vishnu and other gods agreed to Shiva's suggestion and vomited his semen immediately and felt relief from the scorching they had felt earlier. The semen of Shiva was lustrous and golden in colour. It fell on the ground and was so great in quantity that it appeared as if it was touching the heavens.

But Agni was not happy at his state. Shiva gave a separate advice to him and said: "You have committed an improper act by swallowing my semen. Hence your sin has become formidable and that is why the burning sensation you feel has not gone. But now that you have sought refuge in me, I am pleased with you and your misery will soon be over. Go and deposit my semen carefully in the womb of some virtuous woman and you will be relieved of this burning sensation."

Agni replied: "O Lord, this splendour of yours is unbearable. There is no woman in the three worlds except Parvati who can hold it in her womb."

Shiva knew the scorching power of his semen. In order to spare Parvati the discomfort, he said: "Agni, deposit this semen in the bodies of the ladies who take their morning bath in the month of *Magha*."

In the meanwhile, the wives of the seven celestial sages, wanting to take their morning bath came to the river. It was the month of *Magha* and the water of the river was icy-cold. After the bath, six of them felt extremely cold and decided to go near Agni, the fire, to warm themselves. Arundhati, wife of *rishi* Vasishtha, known for her proper conduct and fidelity towards her husband, tried to prevent them from going near Agni as she foresaw the result of it and having realised that the other six wives were deluded and, therefore, feeling cold. But the wives of the six *rishis* stubbornly insisted on going near the fire to warm themselves. As soon as they approached Agni, who had swallowed the semen of Shiva, particles of Shiva's semen entered their bodies through the pores of their hair and Agni was relieved of the burning sensation. After that Agni suddenly vanished in the form of a flame.

The six wives became pregnant and were unhappy at the burning sensation that was caused by the semen. When they went home and their husbands found out about their state, they were furious and, blaming them for infidelity, discarded them. The six ladies were also very unhappy at their own state and they cast off Shiva's semen in the form of a foetus on top of the Himavat mountain and felt relief from the earlier burning sensation. Himavat became scorched from the heat emitting from this foetus and hurled it into the river Ganga. Even Ganga could not bear its heat and deposited it in the forest of Sara grass also called *Sarkanda*, (Erianthus munja) and the foetus became a handsome boy. Thus, on the sixth day of the bright half of the lunar month *Margashirsa*, Shiva's son was born. Sinde the child was born in the forest of *Sara* grass, he was named Skanda. He is also called Visakha, the conquering hero. His epithet is *Shaktidhara* because he conquers all with his spear or *Shakti*. Since the semen of Shiva was cast into the river Ganga and from there finally took the shape of a child, Ganga personified is considered as a consort of Shiva Ganga and Parvati both being the daughters of the Himalaya are considered to be sisters and Shiva's wives.

There are two festivals associated with the river Ganga. One is the festival of her birth celebrated on the 10th bright half of the month of *Jyeshtha*. It is called Ganga Dassehra and heralds the onset of the monsoon. With the monsoon, the waters become turbid and she is called *rajasvala*, like an adolescent girl in her monthly course. After four months, the monsoon is over, the waters begin to clear and then her wedding is celebrated on the 14th day of *Karttika*. Ganga is said to undergo the same course of life from birth to fecundity, as the life of any living creature.

The river Ganga delivers man from the earthly bonds

of matter to the ethereal heights of heaven. And that is why to die or to be cremated on the banks of the Ganga is considered to be highly meritorious.

Skanda, the son of Shiva was nursed by the six discarded wives of the celestial sages who were called *Krittikas* and hence he came to be called Karttikeya. Since the six foster mothers of the child nursed him simultaneously, he developed six heads.

According to a slightly different version of the story, on being approached by the gods and *rishis* for protection against Tarakasura, Shiva plunged his glance into the lake Saravana. From the brilliance of his eyes which looked into the lake, arose six infants who were suckled by the six Krittikas. When Parvati saw the six infants, she embraced them hard and they were squeezed into a single body which, however, retained its six heads. Parvati adopted this child.

Karttikeya developed into a handsome and strong child and when still only seven days old, killed the *asura* Taraka, thus fulfilling the prophecy that only a child of Shiva would kill the demon. Taraka means transparent as well as a star. This is a star which is called the moon. It is a symbol of the mind and represents the mind of the creator. The mind like the moon also has two aspects. It waxes and wanes, is light and dark, it is full of hope and despair. When the mind is under the influence of light, it is intelligent and thinks clearly, but under the influence of darkness, it thinks of evil and is represented by the demon Taraka and that is why he had to be destroyed. Karttikeya killed the demon and cut his body into two pieces. The bigger half became a peacock and Karttikeya took him for his mount. The smaller piece became a cock and Karttikeya used its image for his standard.

Skanda, also called Dhurta is honoured by special ceremonies held in his name on the 6th day of the dark-half of the month of *Phalguna, Ashadha* and *Karttika,* and the name of the festival is Khanda-Maha. He rides either an elephant, a lion, a tiger or a peacock. He holds a spear in his hands and is always accompanied by the Divine Mothers or surrounded by a thousand virgins. He has the title of *Sadyojata* or *Ugra Kumara,* the violent hero.

Originally, Skanda was reckoned as one of the *Pishacha* hosts with an origin from a very low stratum of society. From this low origin, his cult evolved and he was assimilated into the cult of Rudra. At the second stage of development he was assimilated into the cult of Agni and finally into that of Indra. Because of the last assimilation, he was accepted as the husband of Devasena which symbolically is the army of Indra.

Skanda is also called *Bala-graha* or the deity who seizes children. Long ago, blood-sucking creatures were often propitiated by people, so that they would spare their progeny. Skanda was one such *pishacha* who was always accompanied by a team of imps and goblins. Since these *pishachas* were produced from Shiva's seed, they were admitted to the fold of Rudra and came to be called *Rudragana*. And thus Rudra became the begetter of Skanda.

Skanda is also supposed to be a form of fire emanating from Surya, the sun-god. The fire of solar energy mingled with the fire of sacrifice is known as *Avahaniya* fire. Solar fire saw the wives of the seven *rishis* in the *Yajna* and fell in love with them. But his love was not returned. Daksha's wife Svaha, on the other hand, was in love with Agni, the Fire. Assuming the form of the wives of six of the *rishis*, she approached Agni and afterwards threw his semen on a mountainous track full of serpents, *Rakshasas* and *Pishachas*.

Since Agni is a form of Shiva, it is said that Rudra-Shiva and his consort Uma, entered the form of Agni and Svaha, respectively, and Skanda was born as their child. This child had a strange brilliance surrounding him and the Divine Mothers, the *ganas*, the gnomes and tutelary godlings all hastened to pay homage to him. Indra, the god of celestials, seeing this mass homage to a new deity, became alarmed and rushed on his elephant Airavata to kill Skanda. But the child also called Guha, raised such a loud cry that all present were seized with fear. Indra threw his thunderbolt at the child Skanda which hit him on his right side. From this side arose a goat-faced young hero who was named Visakha. Visakha, in other words, was a part of Skanda and, therefore, also a son of Shiva.

Skanda as the leader of the divine forces is called *Senani*.

His vehicle is the peacock and peacocks are the enemies of
snakes. Where a peacock is present, snakes normally do
not exist. And as snakes possess poison, they are a symbol
of death. Therefore, symbolically, the birth of Skanda
signifies that the death-conquering hero has come. But the
body of Skanda's father Shiva is covered with snakes which
signifies that the elements of life and death are reconciled
in Shiva.

GANESHA, THE ELEPHANT-HEADED DEITY

One day, Parvati was surprised by Shiva while she was
taking her bath. Not liking the idea of her privacy being
invaded, she decided to have someone of her own who would
guard her door. So she took the scurf off her body and
kneaded it into the form of a small boy and breathed life
into it. This creature was made a *dvarapala*, the guardian
of her threshold. Forgetting Saturn's malignant eye, Parvati
with a mother's pride, showed him to Saturn. The minute
Saturn looked at Ganesha, the latter's head was burnt to
ashes. Shiva revived Ganesha by putting on his decapitated
body the head of an elephant.

Another story mentions that when Shiva came to his
wife's apartment, Ganesha, the guardian of her door, not only
opposed his entry into her apartment but even had the
audacity to strike him. Infuriated at this behaviour of a
mere *dvarapala*, Shiva ordered his *bhutaganas*, the troops
of demons and imps devoted to him, to kill the *dvarapala*.
But Ganesha managed to check not only the demons but
also the gods who came to the help of the *bhutaganas*. Vishnu
intervened as the honour of the *devatas* was at stake. By
his powers of illusion, he created a ravishingly beautiful
image. Seeing this image of unrivalled beauty, Ganesha was
enchanted for a while and kept looking at it. The *bhutaganas*
and the gods took advantage of this and at an unguarded
moment, struck off Ganesha's head. Parvati was furious at
the death of her son and to take revenge, started fighting
the *devatas*. The celestial troops were frightened at the
intensity of Parvati's fighting and approached the holy sages
to intervene and bring about mediation. Parvati agreed to

make peace but on the condition that the life and head of
her son Ganesha were restored.

Since Parvati refused to compromise on any other terms,
Shiva agreed to bring him back to life and ordered the
devatas to travel north and bring back the head of the first
animal they came across. This happened to be that of an
elephant. With the elephant head placed on his decapitated
body, Ganesha was resuscitated and came to be called
Gajanana, elephant-faced. Shiva was impressed at the fight
that Ganesha had put up and he made him the chief of his
troops the *ganas*, and thus he came to be called *Ganapati*.
Even Shiva is sometimes called Ganapati as he is surrounded
by a host of *ganas*, pramathas or deformed beings. They
represent the human spirit in all its grotesqueness.
Pramatha is a *gana* who is unstable, fleeting, inconstant and
unsteady, conceived as *vighna* implying all impediments,
obstacles and hurdles. This is the *Ghora* or terrible aspect
of a *gana*.

Vighnasura, the genii of obstruction, was created by
Shiva at the request of Indra. Once Prince Abhinandana
offered a great sacrifice and invited all the *devatas* except
Indra. Indra felt insulted and appealed to Shiva to destroy
the sacrifice. Vighanasura was created by Shiva to destroy
the sacrifice of Abhinandana. But after the demon had killed
Abhinandana, he wandered on the earth obstructing all rites,
visible and invisible. The holy sages appealed to Brahma
for protection. Brahma asked them to pray to Ganesha who
alone was before Time and could not be defeated by any
deity. Ganesha was pleased with the devotions of the sages
and defeated Vighnasura. The demon after his defeat
accepted Ganesha as an overlord. This gave Ganesha the
title *Vighnaraja*.

According to another legend, once Shiva and Parvati
turned themselves into a pair of elephants and from their
union was born a child who had an elephant head.

Ganesha is usually invoked as *Vighneshvara*, the lord
of obstacles. Earlier he was propitiated in this form as a
dreaded deity who created obstacles in the fulfilment of man's
desires. But one who creates obstacles is the one who can
also remove them. Later on, *Vighneshvara* was propitiated

so that no obstacles occurred while undertaking new enterprises.

Ganesha is elephant-headed, lion-hearted but rides a rat which in fact is a demon that he once subdued and the demon was forced to take the ignominious shape of a rat. The elephant head is the symbol of an inflated ego. Ganesha is specially propitiated on *Ganesha-chaturthi* which falls on the 4th bright day of the month of *Bhadra*.

WHY GANESHA HAS ONE TUSK

Ganesha is a great gormandizer. One day when the offerings of *Modakas*, the sacrificial cakes, were particularly copious, he could not resist the temptation and kept on eating till he felt uncomfortable. He decided to go for an outing, thinking that fresh air would make him feel better. He mounted his vehicle the rat and the two set out for an excursion to the forest. It was night time. The moon was shining brightly and the sky was studded with stars. In spite of feeling uncomfortable with all the *Modakas* stuffed inside him, Ganesha was in a happy mood and started singing merrily. When they came into the thick of the forest, a snake came out of his hole and crossed their path. This frightened the rat and his tiny legs started shaking, throwing off Ganesha from his back. But the worst was still to happen. Ganesha's belly burst at this shock and all the sacrificial *modakas* rolled out and scattered in the forest. After the initial shock was over, Ganesha gathered his wits and went after the rolling *modakas* and picking them up, stuffed them back into his belly. To prevent the *modakas* in his stomach from falling out through the slit formed as a result of his fall, he caught the snake that was the cause of this mishap and wound him round his belly.

As Ganesha was going to remount the rat, there was a riotous clamour in the sky. Ganesha looked up and saw the moon and his twenty-seven wives, the Constellations, who had witnessed the episode, laughing at him. Feeling insulted, Ganesha removed one of his tusks and, pronouncing a curse, flung it at the moon. The moon was badly hit and turned black and the poor night had to wear mourning for the moon-

light. With perpetual darkness all around, thieves and
criminals abounded. *Devatas* entreated Ganesha, the son of
Parvati, for forgiveness. Ganesha forgave the moon and the
Constellations for making fun of him but only partly. He
avenged the moon for laughing at him and said that there
would be a periodic waning of the moon and that is why
the moon waxes during half the month. Ganesha also had
to suffer and for the rest of his life had to be content with
only one tusk.

A popular legend regarding Ganesha's one tusk is as
follows: Once Shiva and Parvati were resting and Ganesha
was guarding the door. Parashurama, a part incarnation
of Vishnu, came to visit Shiva. He was a great devotee
of Shiva. Ganesha blocked his entry into the celestial
resting-chamber. Parashurama was enraged at the audacity
of the door-keeper and threw his axe at him. Ganesha
recognised the axe as belonging to his father and not wishing
the axe to fall to the ground, he received it on one of his
tusks which broke with the weight of the axe.

Another story connected with his having one tusk says
that Vyasa, compiler of the *Mahabharata*, was dictating the
great epic to Ganesha. Ganesha had no pen to take down
Vyasa's story. So he pulled out one of his tusks and used
it as a pen and that is why he has only one tusk.

Ganesha is also called the god of wit and intelligence
for the following reason: One day, Shiva and Parvati called
their sons Ganesha and Karttikeya and said that they would
marry that son first, who would be the first to return after
going round the world. On hearing these words, Karttikeya
wasted no time and at once set out to go round the world.
But Ganesha, after bowing before his parents, started going
round them from left no right. He circumbulated them seven
times. His parents were surprised at this and asked him
the reason for it. He answered:

"It is written in the *Vedas* that a son who goes seven
times round his parents accrues the merit of going round
the world seven times."

Shiva and Parvati were surprised at Ganesha's wit,
knowledge and intelligence and married him to the two

daughters of Vishvarupa, called Siddhi (success) and Buddhi (wisdom).   Siddhi later gave birth to Kshema and Labha was born to Buddhi.   When Ganesha's brother Karttikeya returned after circumbulating the earth, he was astonished to see his brother who never went round the earth, already married.   He felt cheated and also thought that it was to get him out of the way that such a condition was put by his parents so that Ganesha could be married first.   As a protest, he vowed never to marry and came to be called *Kumara*.   He remained a bachelor but, being the chief of the armed forces, he is said to have married allegorically Devasena, the personified daughter of the army of gods.

4

MAHASHIVARATRI, THE FESTIVAL OF REPENTANCE

When creation had been completed, Parvati asked Shiva which festival in his honour pleased him most and Shiva replied that the festival of Mahashivaratri which fell on the 14th night of the new moon during the dark half of the lunar month of *Phalguna* was his favourite festival.

The three most essential religious activities during the festival are: fasting during the entire lunar day, keeping a strict night vigil and worshipping the *lingam* with offerings of flowers, leaves, cooked food and with recitations of *mantras*. Actually, the time of the festival, i.e., night time, is considered most inauspicious and full of dangers for observing vows and celebrating any festival. But to Shiva, it is the most important time. And in spite of the sinister nature of the time, it is Shiva's favourite time when he takes up residence at places of worship and, therefore, called a *nishachara,* a night-walker. He chooses *bhutas* (ghosts), *Pishachas* (eaters of corpses), and *Kimpurushas* (mongrel men) for his retinue. With this retinue, he roams the cremation-grounds and is, called a *Samshanvasi* one who resides in the burning-ghats. On the night of *Shivaratri* Shiva for the first time had manifested himself in the form of a *linga*. This was done to remove the sins of the world committed during the previous year. The motivation behind the *vrata* or fast is mainly the promotion of physical and mental self-control by acts of penance, thanks-giving and praise of the Supreme Soul or for desiring a special boon.

For the performance of the sacrifice, a three-tiered platform is constructed representing the three levels of the universe. Symbolically, eleven earthen vessels (*kalasha* or *kumbha*), filled with water and representing the eleven forms in which Rudra-Shiva manifests himself to the world, are put on a raised platform where the *Shivaratri* festival is to be performed. Ten of the pots are placed on the middle platform representing the middle region of the universe and these are filled with water, and perfumed with sandalwood and rose water. The arrangement of the pots is two on the eastern side, two on the western, three on the northern and three on the southern. The larger vessel is placed on the highest level of the platform, and since it is considered to be the soul or the essence of the Sun and represents the ethereal regions, it receives the major portion of offerings and oblations.

Each pot is wrapped in a string netting and decorated with leaves of the *Bilva* tree (Aegle marmelos) and mango (Mangifera indica). A coconut is put on the mouth of the pot and the pot is wrapped with a single strip of cloth. The coconut represents the head of the god. This is because the coconut fruit has three black spots on it and Shiva has three eyes. Symbolically, the outer fibrous covering of the fruit represents the matted hair of Shiva and the dark spots, his three eyes. Inside the larger pot, a silver or a golden plate is placed, carved with a *linga*. The *linga* is worshipped by bathing it with the five sacred gifts of the cow called *Panchagavya*, consisting of milk, sour-milk, butter, urine and dung, as well as with the offerings of the five foods of immortality, i.e., milk, curds, ghee, honey and sugar. After the bathing and offering of food ceremonies are over, the *linga* is worshipped by the recitation of sacred *mantras* and by the offering of sesame seeds, grains of rice, boiled rice, and clarified butter. Sacrificial flowers like *Dhattura* (Datura alba) and *Jati* (Murraya paniculata) which are traditionally considered sacred to Shiva, are also offered. During the ceremony, the priests carry a rosary made of *Rudraksha* beads (Eleaocarpus sphaericas).

Symbolism goes a little further and eleven Brahmana

priests sit in a circle around the platform and continuously chant *mantras*. In richer temples, 44 priests divide themselves into four groups of eleven, in keeping with the numerical symbol of eleven and chant eleven times hymns sacred to Rudra-Shiva. Shiva, when thus invoked, takes up residence in the eleven vessels on the altar.

There are thirty-three Vedic gods out of which eleven are Rudras, eight Vasus, twelve Adityas and two Ashwins. The eleven Rudras symbolically are the eleven *pranic* energies which make the universe and individuals function. The wish-fulfiling cow, the daughter of Brahma, is the mother of the eleven Rudras.

These Rudras are considered as manifestations of Shiva, born to *rishi* Kashyapa and Surabhi, the wish-fulfilling cow. According to Siva-Purana, Kashyapa performed severe penances at Kashi and Shiva pleased with him offered him a boon. Kashyapa asked Shiva to always stay at Kashi and he agreed to enter Surabhi and thus were created the 11 Rudras. These Rudras are as follows:

1. *Aja-Ekapad*: The unborn, transcendent creator symbolised as the one-footed goat. It is infinity, a creature without motion or speech. It is also the vehicle of Agni and Agni-Prajapati is also represented as Aja considered as a form of Shiva.

2. *Ahirbudhnya*: Is the dragon of the deep sea, Ahi-Vritra, which lies concealed in primeaval darkness. The dual principles of light and darkness, heat and cold are symbolised as Aja-Ekapad and Ahirbudhnya and these two are in eternal conflict. These two fundamental principles of Fire and Water, Agni and Soma are the two primeaval Rudras.

3. *Tvashtr*: Is the Rudra who fashions the different forms of living creatures. Because of his diversity of forms, he is also called *Bahurupa*. His son is Vishvarupa, also called Trishiras or the one with three heads. The three heads symbolise the threefold creation of life, mind and matter.

4. *Virupaksha*: Shiva, for possessing the third eye. It is a name which means, literally, the eye that creates the different forms.

5. *Raivata*: The word Raivata is after Revati, the presiding constellation of animals and signifies the principle

of nourishment without which no life principle can subsist. He is also called Pushan.

6. *Hara*: Means one that takes life away. In creation, birth and death go side by side and Raivata and Hara as the two forms of Rudra co-exist as the two principles of immortality and death.

7. *Tryambaka*: Is the Rudra with three eyes. It symbolises the various triads on which the entire cosmos is based. Some of the triads are: the three principles of sun, moon and fire; the three states of consciousness: waking state, dreaming state, dreamless state; the three divine mothers, Amba, Ambika, Ambalika who represent the triple vibrations of Mind, Life and Matter but are really the three Fires of the cosmic *Yajna* or Sacrifice.

8. *Savitra*: Is the Rudra who by means of the magic power of words instigates men to act and impel the forces concealed in the transcendent centre to activity. He is symbolised as so many *devas* or divine powers. In the cosmos, Savitra is the sun, the source of heat and light, responsible for generating life. It is one of the names of the sun.

9. *Jayanta* & 10. *Aparajita*: Rudra Jayanta represents the power of Indra and Aparajita that of Vishnu. The two symbolise respectively the centrifugal and the centripetal forces in nature. Jayanta, the victor, is the force moving away from the centre and Aparajita, the unvanquished one, is the force moving towards the centre. The two opposite forces are in constant rivalry and none is defeated and so the world rhythm goes on.

11. *Pinaki*: literally means a bow-wielder. Rudra-Shiva is called *Pinaki* or the wielder of the bow and he shoots his arrows into time as each life has a limited span. It signifies the destructive power of Shiva.

The eleven Rudras are worshipped on the *Ekadashi* day or the eleventh day of the bright and dark halves of the month of *Sawan*. Fasting and propitiating the eleven Rudras are observed on that day.

After the completion of the rites of *Shivaratri*, the devotee presents gifts or donations to the officiating priests and to the other devotees present. According to Vedic scriptures, the performance of this ritual is both obligatory and desirable. The injunctions laid down for the performance of the ritual for transforming the devotee's body into a residence fit for the divinity are: non-injury to living creatures, truthfulness, freedom. from anger, celibacy, compassion, forbearance, austerities, calmness, freedom from passion and malice. As a reward, it is said that one who performs the sacrifice of Shivaratri with all the attendant rituals and keeps the fast according to the rules laid down gets happiness and realises his most cherished desires. He never goes to hell and is liberated from the round of births and deaths. He reaches Shiva's heaven on Mt. Kailash and is accepted as one of his *ganas.*

THE FIVE HEADS OF SHIVA

There were two *daitya* brothers called Sunda and Upasunda. Being very pious, after practising severe penances and undergoing many austerities, they had received the boon of invulnerability from Brahma. According to the boon, they could not die from natural and unnatural causes so long as they were devoted to each other. Sunda and Upasunda were so affectionate and fond of each other that they could not foresee a situation when they could possibly quarrel. Having full confidence in their affection for each other and hence in their invulnerability, they became arrogant and started subduing the inhabitants of the three worlds. Their atrocities reached a stage of non-endurance and the gods, *rishis* and men had to approach Brahma for help. Brahma having earlier given the brothers the boon of invulnerability had now to find a way to bring about discord between them. He thought of many plans and ultimately decided to create a woman of unrivalled beauty as only a woman could bring discord between men. Brahma collected minute particles of all gems and best of all animate beings. He fashioned this mass into the shape of a woman and breathed life into it. This was Tilottama, the celestial damsel, created to beguile the brothers, Sunda and Upasunda. The two brothers who had all along thought and acted together, on seeing her, started fighting. Tilottama was one object that they were not prepared to share. They fought each other for possessing her and ultimately both were killed.

When Tilottama was created, she went round Brahma, Vishnu, Shiva and the *rishis*, in salutation. Seeing such a beautiful damsel, Shiva got enamoured of her and in whichever direction Tilottama turned, a fresh head of Shiva appeared, so that he did not lose sight of her and when Tilottama flew into the heavens, a fifth head appeared on top of his head, facing the heavens and thus was created the five-faced image of Shiva. The fifth head was later lost.

Once Parvati asked Shiva: "Why are your faces that face the east, the north and the west so handsome and agreeable to look at but why is your face turned towards the south so terrible?"

Shiva replied: "With my face turned towards the east, I exercise the sovereignty of the universe. With my face turned towards the north, I sport with you of faultless features. My face turned towards the west is gentle and auspicious and brings happiness to all living creatures. My face turned towards the south is terrible. With it I destroy all creatures.

And thus the four faces of Shiva that appeared out of desire to behold Tilottama came to have different meanings.

The five-faced image of Shiva is called *Panchanama* and mythically his five faces are described as *Pancha-Brahma* which symbolically are: sound, touch, sight, taste and smell. Shiva is the ruler of the five directions of space, of the five human races, the five senses, the five elements and all that is ruled by number five. His five faces are of five different colours. They are pearly or crystalline, yellow, dark blue, white and red. The head facing east is yellow. It is called *Tat-purusha*, the Supreme man. The southern face is blue-black in colour. It is *Aghora*, the non-fearful. The western face is red in colour and is called *Vamadeva*, the left-handed deity. The northern face is *white* called *Sadyoyata*, and the face looking upwards is of *Ishana*, pearly or cystalline in colour, rarely copper-coloured.

Shiva is considered as the entire universe and his five-fold activity is *Srishti* (creation, evolution), *Sthiti* (preservation or support), *Samhara* (destruction, involution), Tirobhava (veiling, deluding) and Anugraha (granting favours and salvation).

THE DESTRUCTION OF THE TRIPURAS

When *Asura* Taraka was killed by Skanda, his three sons
Tarakaksha. Vidyunmali and Kamalaksha performed severe
austerities. The three *asuras* were self-controlled, disciplined,
truthful, of steady mind, heroic but inimical to gods.
Avoiding all enjoyments that captivate the mind, like, the
sound of musical instruments, they disdained all forms of
sensual enjoyment and performed severe austerities.   In
summer they stood amidst blazing fires, in winter in ice-
cold waters and went without food for long stretches of time.
Maintaining strict severity in practising austerities, the
asuras became emaciated by their penances. They stood on
one leg for a hundred years and endured extreme discomfort.
They lived only on air and, for another thousand years, stood
on their heads. Thus, they bore extreme distress in their
intent to conquer all. But all this time their minds were
solely fixed on Brahma.

Satisfied by their penance, Brahma appeared before them
and   offered   them   a   boon.   The   *asuras*   asked   for
indestructability at the hands of everyone.   They said:
"Protect us from our enemies. Let not old age, sickness
or death befall us. Of what avail are riches, vast dominions,
various forms of enjoyments, position and power if death is
the ultimate end? It is futile to live if one is to die at the
end.   Give   us   each   a   strong   city   so   that   we   become
invulnerable."

Brahma agreed to their request but with reservations.
Tarakaksha asked for a golden city, Kamalaksha for a silver
one and Vidhyunmali for a city made of copper. Brahma
ordered Maya, the architect of the *asuras*, to build the three
cities, the golden one in heaven, the silver one in the sky
and the copper one on earth. The condition that Brahma
made for their destruction was that they would be destroyed
only when they came in one line and destroyed by one arrow
shot at the same time.

The three *asura* brothers ruled in their respective cities
for a long time. They lived happily and performed
meritorious deeds. But the celestials were unhappy at the
continuous rule of the *asuras* and requested Brahma to

annihilate them.

Brahma replied: "The asuras have flourished because of my favours. How can I destroy them? Go and pray to Shiva. May be he will accede to your request."

The celestials went and eulogised Shiva for the annihilation of the *asuras*. Shiva appeared before them and said: "The ruler of the *asuras* is a pious person. He who practises meritorious deeds should not be killed. I understand your misery. But the *asuras* are strong and invincible to all except me. They are also my devotees. How can I destroy them? There are ways of atonement and amends for slaying a Brahmana, a wine addict, a thief or one who destroys sacred rites. But there is no expiation for ungratefulness. So long as the *asuras* remain devoted to me, they will not be killed by me."

Shiva is called *Bhaktavatsala* for being favourably disposed towards his devotees. Getting this reply, the celestials went back to Brahma and Vishnu and related all that Shiva had said. Vishnu answered: "It is true that where eternal virtues reign, no misery raises its head. It is like darkness vanishing when the sun rises."

The celestials felt demoralised at Vishnu's reply and answered: "How can we be happy? As long as the Tripuras are alive, we cannot perform virtuous activities. The Tripuras give us trouble. Either they should be destroyed or else the untimely destruction of the celestials will take place."

On seeing the celestials unhappy and distressed, Vishnu thought: "The sons of Taraka are the devotees of Shiva. But I am the benefactor of the celestials. I must do something to make them happy."

He concentrated on the Lord of Sacrifices, the Supreme Soul, without a form. On being meditated upon, the various Sacrifices appeared. Seeing them, the gods according to the rules governing the Sacrifice, worshipped the Sacrificial Being and as a result of it, from the sacrificial pit arose thousands of *bhutas*, i.e., the elements or ghosts. These *bhutas* were armed with various weapons and resembled the destructive fire of Rudra. Vishnu ordered these *bhutas* to burn the three cities of the *asuras* but before they could do that, they themselves got burnt.   Vishnu was very distressed at this and thought:

"The virtuous ones cannot be destroyed by black magic. How can I then destroy their cities? Being devotees of Shiva, they are free from all sin just as the lotus leaf is free of water. I can only destroy them by putting obstacles in the way of their virtuous deeds."

Having realised that so long as the *asuras* worshipped Shiva, they could not be destroyed, Vishnu decided to make the *Vedic dharma* disappear and to make the *asuras* forget the worship of the *lingam*. Having made up his mind, he said to the *devatas*: 'I shall make the *asuras* averse to the worship of Shiva. When Shiva comes to know that they no longer worship him, he will himself reduce them to ashes."

With this in mind, Vishnu started ridiculing the *Vedas* so that the *asuras* would stop worshipping Shiva. He also created a *Purusha*, born of himself who was a delusive creature, a teacher of *Mayamoha* called Arhat and he created a Mayashastra of sixteen *shlokas* in Apabramsha language. He preached the Jain *dharma* to misguide the *asuras*. Mayamoha created four types of preachers for the propagation of this religion. He preached non-violence, forbade *shrauta* and *smarta* rituals discarded the *Varnashrama* system and created an order for women that resulted in their leaving their homes and leading the life of nuns.

Vishnu asked Mayamoha to delude the *asuras* according to the tenets of the deceptive philosophy and to reveal the *tamasic* rites to them so that Shiva would no longer protect them and the three cities could be destroyed.

The ascetic that was created by Vishnu acted in accordance with his orders and he in turn created four disciples all of like form as himself, and he taught them the deceptive cult. All of them had shaven heads, were of auspicious features and followed the heretic cult. They carried a wicker-basket in their hands and covered their mouths with a piece of cloth. They did not talk much except: "*Dharma* is the only true essence of life." They walked very slowly, brushing the ground with a broom made of cloth, afraid even of injuring the lowest of living beings.

Vishnu ordered these men with shaven heads to go to

the desert regions and to stay there, carrying on their duties till the advent of the *kaliyuga*. He advised them thus: "When the *Kaliyuga* begins, reveal the new *dharma*. I promise you protection. No harm will come to you because of your deeds and finally you shall attain *moksha*."

Vishnu entrusted these men to the care of the Preceptor, saying: "Like you, they also belong to me. Their names will have the perfix *Pujya* as they are worthy of respect. They will have epithets like *Rishi, Yati, Acharya* and *Upadhaya* as appendages to their names."

The deceptive sage accompanied by his disciples went to the three cities of the *asuras* with intent to destroy them but his efforts were unsuccessful because the *asuras* worshipped Shiva. The heretic sage mentally eulogised Vishnu, and Vishnu in turn remembered Narada by the process of thought-forms, and immediately Narada appeared before Vishnu and with due reverence asked what the orders were for him.

Vishnu replied: "Narada, go to the Tripuras. The heretic sage has gone there to delude the residents of the three cities and you must help him."

Narada proceeded to where the ascetic, expert in magic art was, and together they entered the cities of the *asuras*. Narada first got himself initiated into the new religion and then approached the ruler of the Tripuras and said to him: "A very virtuous sage has arrived. He possesses complete knowledge of the *Vedic* lore. I have studied many cults but none has been so good as compared to this one. Seeing the eternal virtue of this cult, I have got myself initiated into it. If you like, you can also get yourself initiated into it."

On hearing Narada speak so highly of the new cult, the ruler of the Tripuras said: "Since Narada has got himself initiated into the new cult, it must be really good. And I think we too shall get ourselves initiated into it." He approached the new sage and asked him to perform his initiation as he wished to become his disciple.

At these words of the ruler of the Tripuras, the heretic sage said with emphasis: "I shall only initiate you if you are prepared to act according to my behests and not otherwise."

The *asura* chief answered: "I will not go contrary to your orders and will carry out whatever command you are pleased to give."

The sage, thus assured by the *asura* chief, performed the initiation of the three brothers according to the cult rites.   When the residents of the three cities saw their masters embrace the new religion, they also decided to do the same. At the end of the initiation ceremony of the *asuras*, the sage gave a discourse to them and said:

"The entire universe is eternal. It has no creator nor is it an object of creation. It evolves itself and gets annihilated by itself. There are no gods, only bodies with different names. All the bodies from that of Brahma to that of a mosquito perish when their time arrives. All living beings eat, drink, sleep, copulate, make merry, derive kindred satisfaction and, when their time comes, perish. The fear of death is the same from Brahma to the worm and there is no virtue equal to the virtue of showing mercy to living beings. If a single living being is protected, it amounts to the protection of the three worlds; if that is killed, it amounts to the killing of all others. Hence it is one's duty to protect and abstain from killing. Non-violence is the greatest virtue. Affliction of others is a great sin. There is no sin equal to violence in the whole of the universe. A man who is violent and kills others goes to hell and a non-violent person goes to heaven.

"There is no gift equal to that of protection. There are four types of gifts mentioned by the sages. They are: Protection of the frightened, medicine for the sick, learning to be imparted to the student and food given to the hungry. Heaven and hell are here only. Happiness is heaven and misery is hell.

"The *Vedic* text encouraging slaughter of animals cannot be held authoritative by the learned. It is strange that the *Vedas* recommend slaughtering of animals, and burning of gingely seeds and clarified butter to attain heaven. The *Vedas* also mention that the human body is ultimately going to constitute the food of dogs, crows and worms and its ultimate end is to be reduced to ashes. But still the people are divided into different castes. The four castes of the

Hindus are believed to come from different parts of Brahma.
But how can sons born of the same body be of different
castes?"

After addressing the *asuras* thus, the sage criticised the
womanly virtue of chastity and the manly virtue of
continence as given in the sacred texts. He also criticised
the rites of *shraddha*, ceremonial ablutions, charitable gifts,
sacrifices, anniversaries, etc. He repudiated the worship of
Shiva, Vishnu, Surya, Ganesha and other deities.

The influence the sage wielded over the *asuras* resulted
in a complete stoppage of *Vedic* rites in the three cities of
the *asuras*. The women stopped being devoted to their
husbands, the men started seducing women. Thus when the
citizens became averse to virtuous rites and actions, evil
reigned all over. At the bidding of Vishnu, evil fortune
visited the three cities. Law and order disappeared and the
authority of the rulers was gone.

Now that the *asuras* were no longer propitiating Shiva,
the deities asked for the destruction of the Tripuras. Pleased
with the devotion of the *devatas,* Shiva granted their wish
and to carry out the gigantic task of destroying the three
cities, he commissioned Vishvakarman, the celestial
architect, to build him a chariot in which he could go to
the three cities and destroy them.

THE CHARIOT OF SHIVA

For building Shiva's divine chariot, the entire universe
was commissioned and all the elements, rivers, mountains,
sun, moon, stars, earth, etc., went into the making of the
chariot. The chariot was golden in colour, its right wheel
was the sun and the left wheel was the moon. The right
wheel had twelve spokes presided over by the twelve Adityas.
The left wheel had sixteen spokes consisting of sixteen digits
of the moon with its asterisms embellished on it. The six
seasons constituted the rim of the wheel. The sky formed
the *Pushkara* of the chariot and Mt. Mandara formed the
inner side of the chariot, the rising and setting suns
constituted the pole-shafts. Mahamara was its support and
the Kesara mountains its sharp sides. The days of the year

constituted its velocity, the northern and southern *Ayanas* constituted the junctions of the wheels and axles. The *Muhurtas* formed the joints and the *Kalas* the pin of the yoke. The division of time, called Kashtha, constituted the nose of the chariot and the *kshanas*, the axle-shaft. *Nimesas* formed the bottom of the carriage and the minutest division of time the poles. The firmament constituted the fender of the chariot, heaven and salvation, the flag-staffs. Abhramu and Kamadhenu, its harrows which were at the end of the shafts. The unmanifest principle formed their shaft and cosmic intellect, the chariot's reeds; cosmic ego and cosmic elements, its strength. Cosmic sense-organs formed the embellishments of the chariot. Faith was its movement, the six *Vedangas*, its ornaments. Good rites, *puranas, nyaya, mimamsas, dharma-shastras* were its side ornaments and the *mantras*, its tinkling bells. The serpent Ananta with its thousand hoods formed its fittings, the main and subsidiary quarters and the pedestals of the chariot. The bright-coloured clouds called Pushkara formed the jewel-studded banners and the four oceans were the bullocks of the chariot. Ganga and other rivers in their anthropomorphic female forms held the fly whisks in their hands. The seven winds called *Avaha* which circulate between *Bhuloka* and *Svargaloka* constituted the steps of gold leading to the chariot. The *Lokaloka* mountains bounding the seven seas and dividing the visible from the region of darkness, formed its side steps, and lake Manasa, its outer and oblique steps. The Varsha mountains formed the cords and chains around the chariot and all the residents of the *Tala* region, the undercarriage of the chariot.

Brahma was the charioteer and the gods were the holders of the bridle, the *Vedic* divinities formed *Pranava*, the whip of Brahma. The syllable A formed the umbrella of the god. The Lord of the mountains became his bow and the Lord of the serpents, the bow-string.

Saraswati, in the form of the *Vedas*, constituted the bells of the bow. Vishnu became the arrow and Agni formed the spear-head of the arrow. The four *Vedas* became the horses and the planets became their embellishments. Winds formed the feathers of the chariot and water his army. The celestial *rishis* pushed the vehicle.

After the divine chariot was ready, the *Vedas* were harnessed as horses. The gods, *gandharvas, nagas, rishis,* Vishnu, Brahma and the *Lokapalas* eulogised Shiva, and Brahma requested him to mount it. When Shiva mounted the chariot, the horses, which were really the *Vedas,* fell to the ground, the earth-quaked, the mountains trembled, bringing about a great upheaval and *Shesha,* the divine snake, was unable to bear the weight of the earth on his back. To save the situation, Vishnu took the form of a bull, went under the chariot and lifted it on his back and tried to steady the universe. But even he could not bear the weight of Shiva and had to kneel down. Shiva then merely touched the bridle, the horses steadied and Brahma could then drive the chariot with the velocity of wind and mind, and went towards the three cities of the *asuras.*

Before the chariot reached the three cities of the *asuras,* Shiva addressed the gods and said: "The *asuras* can only be killed after separate animal hoods have been assigned to the *devatas* and other beings. All of you give me the lordship of the animals, so that I can kill the Tripuras.

The *devatas* became suspicious on hearing this. Shiva realised their suspicions and hesitations and said: "By declaring yourselves as mere *pashus,* i.e., animals, you will not fall from grace. Later on you can practise penances for release from your animalhood. He who performs the divine rite of *Pashupata* will he released from his animalhood."

Thus addressed by Shiva, Brahma, Vishnu and *devatas,* agreed and declared themselves as mere *pashus* or animals, and Shiva became *Pashupati,* the Lord of animals. *Pashupati* unties the noose of animals and gives them release from their animal nature after which they become *sattva* or pure and their souls find *moksha.* But before the gods could attain the final release, they had to observe the difficult *Pashupata vrata.* According to the *Pashupata-sutras, Pashupati* is the only cause and he grants his grace directly and ends one's sorrows. There are only three realities, i.e., *pati* (god), *pashu* (ego) and *pasha* (bondage). These are the three qualities: perception, inference and authority.

Shiva as *Pashupati* is the lord of all sentient beings. And beings are bound by cause and effect, the sense-objects to which they are attached. Unless the *pasha* or the bonds are broken by the grace of Shiva, no one can get rid of them and the soul remains bound in the snare of death. The bonds known as *Indrajala* or *Shakrajala* are the five elements of gross matter which snare and tie an individual to earthly pleasures. *Pashupati* is the Creator, Preserver and Destroyer of the universe and his various names are *Vama, Deva, Jyestha, Rudra.*

THE BURNING OF THE TRIPURAS

Shiva, now equipped with everything, sat in the chariot and got ready to burn down the three cities. He strung his bow and fixed the arrows but the three cities did not come within the target path of Shiva which was the condition laid down for their destruction. Shiva heard a voice from the firmament:

"You cannot kill the Tripuras as long as you do not offer worship to Ganesha the god who removes all obstacles."

Ganesha was sitting on Shiva's right side. Shiva offered him worship and immediately after that, the three cities of the *asuras* joined together in one unit. At this, the gods, *siddhas* and *rishis* raised a tumultuous roar of joy and Brahma and Vishnu requested Shiva to discharge his arrow. "The time for killing the *asuras* has arrived." they said. "The three cities have come into one unified whole. Please discharge your arrow and reduce them to ashes before they separate again."

Shiva had earlier been very attached to the *asuras* as they were his devotees and did not wish to destroy them. But since they had turned away from the right path, he had no choice left. However, at the thought of their impending destruction, he shed tears. The tears of Shiva (Rudra) turned into beads called *Rudraksha* (Eleocarpus sphaericus) which are till today held sacred by his followers.

Shiva steadied himself. He strung the bow tight and fixed the arrow *Pashupata* and concentrating on the Tripuras in the auspicious moment called *Abilasha*, he drew the bow.

The bow made an unbearable twanging sound, and the arrow with the refulgence of countless suns was discharged. The arrow was formed of Vishnu with its head of Agni, the god of fire. It blazed through the three cities and, along with its inhabitants, reduced it to ashes. This was made possible because the *asuras* had refrained from worshipping Shiva. Just as the universe is burnt at the end of a *kalpa*, so everything and everyone was destroyed. Not even a minute particle except Maya, the imperishable architect of the *asuras*, escaped unscathed in the simultaneous destruction of the three cities. Shiva henceforth came to be called *Tripurari* or *Tripuntkara*.

The three cities of the *asuras* made of the three base elements of gold, silver and copper are conceived as the level of mind, vital airs and material element of man. These are symbolised as the demon Tripura who could only be killed by a single shaft struck from the bow of Shiva. This arrow is symbolised as the central nervous system. Just as the three cities of the *asuras* could be brought under control by Shiva's arrow, similarly the human mind and body can be controlled by the control of the senses. The central nervous system is the Golden Rod or Axis of the human body, also called *Sumeru* or *Pinaka*.

The region of Mandhata in the Narmada valley was specially connected with demon legends. This is believed to be the *daitya* stronghold of Tripura and of the demon Mahisha, after whom the towns of Tewar and Mahesar are said to have been named.

The Narmada and Tapti Valleys in western India are considered to be the earlier strongholds of Shiva worship and six out of the twelve Jyotir *linga* shrines are situated in this region. They are:

1. Omkara (Amreshvara) in mandhata on the south bank of the river Narmada, Madhya pradesh.
2. Mahakala at Ujjain, Madhya pradesh.
3. Tryambaka at Nasik, on the banks of river Gautami, Maharashtra
4. Ghrneshvara at Ellora, Maharashtra
5. Naganath, east of Ahmednagar, Maharashtra
6. Bhima-Shankar at the source of river Bhima, Maharashtra

5

SOME INTERESTING LEGENDS

WHY DRAUPADI HAS FIVE HUSBANDS

According to a story narrated in the *Mahabharata*, Draupadi in an earlier age was the daughter of a *rishi*. Having remained unmarried, she propitiated Shiva for the boon of a husband. Pleased with her austerities, Shiva appeared before her and offered her a boon. She asked for a husband and, in her eagerness to get married, she made the request five times and each time Shiva agreed to give her a husband. But when she realised that she was going to get five husbands, she protested, but in spite of her objections, Shiva stuck to his word. That is why in another age, she was born as Drupada's daughter and married the five Pandava brothers.

According to a different version, the reason for Draupadi to have five husbands was that once Indra went to Mt. Himavat and accosted Shiva rudely. To teach him a lesson, Shiva merely pointed to a cave in the mountains where four earlier Indras were kept and said that he along with the four earlier Indras would be born on earth as human beings, in order to reduce the over-population of the world, and that Lakshmi would be born as their common wife. In later texts, Lakshmi was substituted by Indrani, the wife of Indra. Because of Indra's arrogance and audacity in accosting Shiva, five portions of his essence became incarnate in the five Pandava brothers and his wife Indrani became incarnate as Draupadi, so that she was still the wife of only one man.

USHA FALLS IN LOVE WITH ANIRUDDHA

Usha, the beautiful daughter of Bana, the king of the *asuras*, ruler of Tezpur in Assam, was once staying as a guest of Shiva and Parvati. Bana, who was a great devotee of Shiva, had in fact given his daughter in adoption to Parvati. Shiva, pleased with Bana's devotions, had given him one thousand arms which made him almost invulnerable.

Once Usha saw Parvati in an amorous dalliance with Shiva and this evoked amorous thoughts in her too and she also wished to have a husband. Parvati guessed her thoughts and gave her a boon of a husband. When Usha asked who her husband was going to be, Parvati answered:

"On the twelfth day of the bright half of *Vaishakh*, you will see a youth in your dreams and he shall be your husband."

Soon after this episode, Parvati deputed Usha to look after her minor son Ganesha while she went for a bath. The two children soon got engrossed in play and did not notice Shiva coming. Shiva was in an agitated state of mind and wished to enter his wife's apartment. Ganesha had been asked by Parvati not to let anyone enter her apartments while she was having a bath. Seeing Shiva almost at the threshold of Parvati's apartments, Ganesha rushed and prevented him from entering. This infuriated Shiva who was already in a bad temper and in anger he decapitated Ganesha. His head was later replaced with that of an elephant. Usha, who witnessed all this, got frightened and in fear of Shiva's wrath, hid in a barrel of salt.

Parvati vented her wrath on Usha for Ganesha's fate, whose negligence, she said, resulted in Ganesha having the head of an elephant and cursed her to be born on earth. Usha asked to be forgiven, saying that on earth she would die unrecognised. But since a curse once pronounced could not be completely withdrawn, Parvati modified it and said that in her honour no salt would be taken during the month of *Chaitra,* and instead food would be seasoned with the juice of tamarind. (Tamarindus indica.)

Soon after this curse was pronounced on her, Usha was reborn on earth. When she grew into a young maiden, she saw a handsome youth in her dreams and fell in love with him. But when on waking, she did not see him, she got very upset and confided her dream to her friend and constant companion, Chitralekha. Chitralekha was an expert in drawing. Seeing her friend in distress, she sketched for her the faces of many young men. One of them Usha recognised as that of the youth she had seen in her dream. Chitralekha, for her friend's sake, concentrated her mind and saw the young man residing at Dwaraka with his grandfather Krishna. By her magic powers, Chitralekha brought this young man called Aniruddha into the palace of Usha.

Before all this took place, Banasura had been engaged in the adoration of Shiva. He prayed to Shiva: "I feel humiliated at possessing a thousand arms when there is peace all around. Without war, what is the use of these arms? They are only a burden to me. Let hostilities start, so that I may benefit from them".

Shiva replied: "When your peacock banner is broken, then there will be a war."

Bana was pleased with this prophecy and thanking Shiva, returned to his palace where he found his standard broken, seeing which his joy increased.

About that time, Chitralekha returned from Dwaraka, bringing Aniruddha with her. The guards of Usha's palace, finding a youth in her apartment, informed Banasura. The *asura* chief immediately sent his soldiers to seize Aniruddha but the valiant prince slew his assailants with an iron club. Bana himself attacked him but Aniruddha could not be subduded. Bana had to use his magic faculties and succeeded in capturing the prince and bound him by serpent cords.

When Aniruddha was missed from Dwaraka, a search for him started but there was no trace of him anywhere. Finally, *rishi* Narada came and told Krishna of what had happened and how Aniruddha was a prisoner of Bana. Hearing this, Krishna, accompanied by his brother Balarama and son Pradyumna, the father of Aniruddha, set out for the city of Bana. When they approached the city, the spirits attending on Rudra, opposed them but they were soon destroyed by Vishnu. On reaching the city, a mighty Fever, a personification of an emanation of Shiva Maheshwara, attacked them. This personified Fever had three feet and three heads. Balarama, upon whom his ashes were scattered, was seized with burning heat and his eyelids trembled, but he felt relief from the burning fever when he clung to the body of Krishna. The body of Krishna also emanated a fever and the two fevers fought each other till the Great Fever of Shiva's body was absorbed within Shiva. Next Vishnu overcame the army of the *Danavas*. Bana with his *daitya* host and assisted by Shiva and Skanda, fought Vishnu. A fierce battle took place between Vishnu and Shiva. The earth quaked and the three worlds were scorched by the flaming weapons hurled, giving the impression that the end of the universe was at hand. Shiva was defeated in the battle and Skanda, the god of war, was badly wounded and fled from the battlefield. Bana attacked Krishna. The two threw fiery weapons at each other which pierced their armour but Krishna intercepted the arrows of Bana and cut them to pieces. After a while, Krishna decided to put Bana to death. He picked up his *Sudarshana chakra* which was blazing with the radiance of a thousand suns and was about to cast it at Bana. Seeing Krishna with the Discus in his hand, ready to kill Bana, Shiva addressed Krishna:

"O Krishna, I know your might. You are the Supreme Lord. I have given Bana assurance of safety. Please do not falsify what I have said. He has grown old in devotion to me. Let him not incur your displeasure."

Thus addressed Krishna, looked graciously at Shiva, and answered: "Since you have given a boon to Bana, let him live. Because I respect your wishes, I will withdraw my Discus. The assurance of safety granted by you to Bana is also granted by me. That which I am, you are and that also is this world with all its inhabitants. Men contemplate distinctions between us because they are stupefied by ignorance."

So saying, Krishna went to the place where Aniruddha had been kept a prisoner. Taking Aniruddha and Usha with him on his mount Garuda, and accompanied by Balarama and Pradyumna, he returned to Dwaraka where Usha's marriage with Aniruddha was solemnised.

THE DESTRUCTION OF JALANDHARA

Lavanambhodhi, the ocean of salt, at the confluence of the river Sindhu and the Arabian Sea, popularly called *Sindhu-sagara-sangama,* was the place where Shiva cast the effulgence from his third eye and it took the form of a child. This child cried so lustily that it created earthquakes and the noise made by him defeated even the *satyaloka* of Brahma. His crying was so loud that it frightened the inhabitants of the three worlds and the celestials and sages being distressed, sought refuge in Brahma.

To find out the cause of the uproar, Brahma descended to the earth and along with his entourage of celestials, went towards the source of the noise. There he saw this child floating on the waters of the ocean. The ocean, on seeing Brahma himself grace his abode, assumed the form of a god and bowing before him, placed the child in his lap. Brahma asked the ocean about the parentage of the child but the ocean was unable to give an answer and said:

"O Brahma, this child suddenly appeared at the confluence of the river Sindhu and the sagara. I do not know about his parentage. You perform his post-natal rites and tell me about the predictions regarding his future."

The Ocean had barely finished speaking when the child caught hold of Brahma's neck and shook it so severely that tears came out of Brahma's eyes.

Brahma, after extricating himself from the child's grip, said: "Since he made my eyes water, he will be famous by the name of Jalandhara." and then casting the child's horoscope, he added, "This boy will attain youth immediately. He will master the sacred texts and will be courageous, heroic and majestic. He will become the ruler of the *asuras,* conquer many lands and will shine with glory. He will have a chaste and beautiful wife who will increase his fortune. He will be invincible to all except Shiva and after his death, he will return to wherever he has come from."

Jalandhara, instead of taking the normal course of growing up, immediately became a young man and Shukra, the priest of the *asuras,* performed his coronation. He was brought up as a son of Varuna, the Ocean, and the latter requested *asura* Kalanemi to give his daughter Vrinda in marriage to Jalandhara. Vrinda was the great, great, granddaughter of Hiranyakashipu. Kalanemi agreed to the proposal and Vrinda was married to Jalandhara. Jalandhara ruled piously for many years and performed many pious deeds and penances. Pleased with him, Brahma gave him a boon. Jalandhara asked for invulnerability from all, so long as his wife Vrinda remained faithful to him, and Brahma agreed.

Once when Jalandhara and his wife Vrinda were sitting along with the other *asuras,* their priest Shukra arrived. Jalandhara asked Shukra the reason why Rahu, the son of Viprachitti and Simhika, was headless. Shukra related to him the story of the churning of the Milky Ocean: "Once there was a strong hero called Bali, the great grandson of Hiranyakashipu," he said. "He was a virtuous ruler but the *devatas* having been defeated by him were unhappy. They, along with Indra, took refuge in Vishnu. At the suggestion of Vishnu, the *devatas*, clever at deception, made an alliance with the *asuras* to churn the Ocean of Milk to extract nectar. The *devatas*, who are the traditional enemies of the *asuras*, extracted many jewels from the ocean and kept them for themselves. Among the articles churned out of the ocean was the celestial elephant Airavata, which Indra took for his mount, Lakshmi whom Vishnu took as his wife, the crescent moon which adorns the forehead of Shiva and many other articles. But last of all came the deadly poison Kalakuta which Shiva drank to save the universe from untimely annihilation. Parvati afraid for his life held his throat tight so that the poison stayed there and gave Shiva a blue throat and the epithet *Neela-kantha*. *Amrita*, the drink of immortality, which was churned out of the ocean, was drunk by them selfishly, deceiving the *asuras* and depriving them of their share. But Rahu somehow managed to take a little bit of the drink of immortality. Vishnu , who is always a partisan of Indra, in revenge, cut off his head."

Jalandhara became furious at hearing the story of the churning of the Ocean which was his father. His eyes turned red with anger and he sent his emissary Ghasmara to Indra.

Ghasmara hastened to *Trivishtapa*, the city of Indra on Mt. Meru and entered *Sudharama*, the assembly hall where Indra and all the celestials were assembled. He spoke haughtily before the assembled gathering and addressing Indra said: "Jalandhara the son of the Ocean is the lord and Emperor of the *asuras*. I, Ghasmara, am his emissary."

After introducing himself, he repeated the exact words of Jalandhara. "O base god, why was my father churned by you with Mt. Mandara as the churning stick and the celestial serpent Vasuki as the churning rope? Why were all the jewels of my father taken away? Return to me the jewels that are my patrimony or run the risk of complete annihilation at my hands."

Indra answered: "The reason for churning the Ocean and taking away the jewels was that the Ocean had given shelter to the mountains who were afraid of me and had also saved and sheltered my enemies, the *asuras*."

Ghasmara hastened back to Jalandhara and conveyed to him Indra's reply. Jalandhara's lips throbbed with anger and desirous of conquering the *devatas*, he set forth with his army and heroic generals like Shumbha and Nishumbha. His army camped at Nandana. Jalandhara blew his conch and his soldiers roared like lions. Finding his favourite city of Amaravati surrounded by *asuras*, Indra organised his army to fight.

The celestials and demons rushed against each other with iron clubs, arrows, maces, axes and spears. The ground was red with the blood of the slain and the dust raised gave the impression of dusk with the clouds scattered all around.

Shukra with his *sanjivani-vidya* brought back to life the *asuras* killed in the battle and Brihaspati resuscitated the celestials killed in the battle, with divine herbs from Mt. Drona.

When Jalandhara saw the celestials being restored to life, he spoke angrily to Shukra: "How do the celestials killed by me rise again? No one but you have the *sanjivani-vidya*."

Shukra told Jalandhara that Brihaspati was bringing the divine herbs from Mt. Drona and reviving them and suggested to Jalandhara to uproot the mountain and hurl it far into the Ocean.

Thus addressed by his preceptor, Jalandhara hastened

to the lofty mountain, uprooted it with his strong hands and hurled it into the Ocean. Accompanied by a vast army, he came back to the battlefield and began to kill the celestials. On seeing the celestials being killed, Brihaspati went to gather the divine herbs from Mt. Drona. Not finding the mountain there, he realised that the *asuras* had removed it. He was terrified at the possible outcome and worried at the thought of the final destruction of the *devatas*, he hurried to them, "O *devatas*, run away", he advised. "There is no trace of the mountain Drona. It must have been destroyed by the *asuras*. Jalandhara cannot be defeated as he is a part of Shiva himself."

On hearing the words of their preceptor, the celestials abandoned all hopes of victory. Losing courage, they became terrified and fled in all directions. On seeing the celestials routed, Jalandhara with sounds of victory, blowing of conches and beating of drums, entered the city of Amravati. At the same time, Indra and the celestials took refuge in the caverns of Mt. Meru.

Leaving Shumbha in charge of his forces at Amravati, Jalandhara himself entered the caverns of Mt. Meru. Seeing him come personally, the *devatas* including their king Indra, trembled with fear and fled away. With Brahma as their leader, they went to Vishnu and eulogised him. Vishnu in answer to their prayers replied: "Since I have been approached by you, I will certainly ask Jalandhara to stop hostilities against the celestials. But I am warning you that at best I can only show my valour to him and not kill him as he is a part of Shiva.

Vishnu mounted his vehicle, Garuda and accompanied by Indra and other celestials, hastened to fight the *asuras*. Jalandhara asked his army to put up a stiff fight. The battle lasted a long time but there was no sign of the *asuras* being defeated. The celestials felt disheartened at this and once again fled from the battlefield. This infuriated Vishnu and he started killing the *asuras* with vengeance. Seeing his men being killed, Jalandhara also rushed to the scene and personally fought with Vishnu. The battle between the two was severe, the arrows discharged by them filled the sky and the noise made by the twang of the bow of Vishnu filled everyone with fear but Jalandhara remained invincible. Vishnu was impressed with Jalandhara's valour and asked him to choose a boon. Jalandhara addressed Vishnu who was in a way his brother-in-law as Lakshmi, the wife of Vishnu, was also born of the Ocean and therefore, a sister of Jalandhara, and said: "O brother-in-law, if you are pleased with me, stay in my house along with Lakshmi and your followers."

Vishnu agreed and went to live with Jalandhara in his city of the same name. Jalandhara ruled over the three worlds virtuously and appointed his *asura* chiefs in the posts previously held by the celestials. He confiscated the gems hoarded by the *devatas, gandharvas* and *siddhas.*

Even though the *asuras* were ruling the earth virtuously, the confiscation of their property and their being reduced to the position of slaves, made the *devatas* very unhappy and they sought refuge in Shiva. Shiva, known for fulfilling the desires of his devotees, commissioned Narada to help the celestials as Vishnu had started living with Jalandhara. Narada promised to help the *devatas* and, after consoling them, went to the assembly chamber of Jalandhara where he was hospitably received. After the usual formalities were over, Jalandhara asked him the reason for his visit.

Narada answered: "O Lord of the *Danavas* and *daityas,* you are the enjoyer of all the jewels and the ruler of the three worlds. I recently visited Mt. Kailash which has a grove of *kalp trees* which fulfils every wish. It has a divine brilliance, illuminated by *chintamani* gems and gold. Hundreds of *Kamadhenus* graze there. There I saw the handsome, fair-complextioned Shiva with his three eyes and with the crescent moon on his forehead, seated with Parvati. On seeing such a wonderful sight, I wondered if such splendour was to be found elsewhere. I had heard of your prosperity and wondered if it matched with that of Shiva and came personally to see it."

On hearing these words of Narada, Jalandhara proudly took him round his dominion and showed him his possessions. Narada, in the interest of the celestials, tried to make Jalandhara jealous and said: "Jalandhara, you have everything that is conducive to prosperity. You are the Lord

of the three worlds. You possess jewels, gems, elephants,
mansions. Indra's elephant Airavata and the sun's horse
Ucchaihshravas is yours, the celestial *Kalpataru* (*Kalpa* tree),
the treasures of Kubera and the aerial chariot of Brahma
yoked to the swan belong to you. In fact, all the excellent
things available in heaven, earth and the nether-worlds
flourish in your mansions. I am delighted to see your great
affluence but your mansion is deficient in one respect. You
do not possess the most excellent of ladies. One who
possesses everything but does not possess the most excellent
of ladies, his life is rendered waste and he does not shine."

Jalandhara's passion was roused by this and he said: "I
bow to thee, Narada. Tell me where is this most excellent
of ladies to be found. If such a lady exists anywhere in
the universe, I swear, she shall be mine."

Narada answered: "On the summit of Mount Kailash,
Shiva lives assuming the form of a naked *yogi* along with
his wife Parvati who is an exquisitely beautiful woman. Such
a perfect beauty incites the passions of everyone and
fascinates even the *yogis*. Even Brahma lost his equilibrium
on seeing her, and Shiva, reputed to be free from infatuation,
has been won over by her feminine charms. There is none
more prosperous than Shiva in the whole universe, for he
possesses the most excellent of ladies. The prosperity that
he enjoys because of his dalliance with her has not come
to you in spite of your being the master of so much wealth."
Inciting Jalandhara, Narada departed.

After Narada left, Jalandhara became restless and almost
lost his equilibrium. Parvati's beauty haunted him. He
was harassed with thoughts of lust for her and decided to
possess her, no matter what the cost. Having lost his clear
thinking and swayed by Time, the annihilator, he called his
messenger and asked him to take his message to Shiva.

"O Shiva, of what use is an exquisitely beautiful wife
to you, you who stay in jungles and are attented upon by
ghosts, goblins and spirits? I am the ruler of the three worlds
and enjoy all excellent things. All the mobile beings and
immobile objects are under my suzerainty. I have seized
the elephant of Indra, the horse Ucchaihshravas and the
celestial Parijata tree (Nyctanthes arbor-tristis). Brahma's

chariot, fitted with the divine swan, stands in my courtyard. The treasures of Kubera are in my custody, the umbrella of Varuna sheds brilliance in my house, the noose of Varuna and the garland of never-fading flowers is mine. The javelin *Mrityu* (death) has been seized by me and Agni, the God of Fire, has given me two sets of clothes purified by the holy fire. Since all excellent things shine in my possession, O ascetic with matted hair, you also surrender your wife to me. How can the auspicious daughter of Himavat be a wife to you who habitually stay in the cremation grounds, wearing garlands of bones and skulls and assuming the form of a naked ascetic?"

When Rahu gave this message of Jalandhara to Shiva, Shiva's anger took the form of a terrible looking creature which came out of the space between the eyebrows of Shiva. This creature had the face of a lion and flames were coming out of his eyes. His body was dry and rough to the touch, his hair stood on end, his arms were long with stout calves and with a tongue that was lolling out with hunger. He came rushing at Rahu, ready to devour him. Rahu was terrified and rushed to Shiva for protection.

Shiva addressed his *Gana* and said, "Leave off this emissary of Jalandhara. Those who seek shelter shall be protected and not punished.'

Commanded thus by Shiva, the *gana* set Rahu free and then pleaded with Shiva: "O deity favourable to his devotees, my prey has been denied to me, I am tormented by hunger. What shall I eat? Give me food."

Shiva replied: "If you are so badly in need of food, then eat the flesh of your own hands and feet."

Thus commanded, the Gana ate the flesh from his limbs and body till he was left with only his head. Shiva was pleased that he obeyed his commands so implicitly and said:

"O excellent one! I am pleased with this action of yours. You are blessed by me since you carried out my behest to the very letter. I appoint you, therefore, as my door-keeper and order that you create terror for all wicked people. You are my favourite creation and I ordain that you shall be worshipped along with my worship. Henceforth you shall be known as *Kirtimukha*."

Rahu was then let off in the country of Barbaras, identified as Abhira, the Abir desh, somewhere in the south-west of the Indus delta. Considering himself as reborn. Rahu's pride was humbled and he made his way to Jalandhara's city without wasting any time and there informed the *daitya* chief of the conversation that had taken place. This infuriated the *Daitya* even further and he commanded his entire army to fight the *ganas* of Shiva. As soon as he gave the command, the sky became over-cast and many ill omens appeared which portended annihilation all around. *Devatas* got frightened at this and, led by Indra, sought refuge in Shiva. They informed Shiva that even Vishnu who had been assigned the task of getting rid of the *daityas* and make the universe a safe place to live had failed, as Vishnu was living with Jalandhara.

Shiva was surprised to hear this news and sent for Vishnu. He asked Vishnu the reason for failing in his assigned duty. Vishnu replied: "Jalandhara could not be killed by me because he is born of you. Besides he is Lakshmi's brother and I could not kill my brother-in-law."

Shiva told the *devatas* that he himself would rid the universe of Jalandhara as all other efforts had been in vain and assured them that they need not fear any more.

In the meanwhile, *daityas* laid seige to Mount Kailash. Shiva was furious at the tumultuous roar made by them and ordered his *ganas* to get ready for battle. A tough battle took place between the *daityas* and Shiva's *ganas*. The *ganas* descended from Mount Kailash shouting war-cries. Weapon clashed with weapon. The earth shook with the sounds of war drums and the battlefield was strewn in no time with javelins, clubs, arrows, maces and pikes. The *daityas* killed by the Pramathas and the *ganas* were again and again resuscitated by Shukra. The terrified *ganas* intimated Shiva about the *daityas* being brought back to life. Hearing this, Shiva was furious and a terrible form called *Kritya* came out of his mouth. Her calves were stout as palmyra trees, her mouth was huge and deep like mountain caverns. She rushed fearlessly into the battlefield and started devouring the *asuras*. She was so big and strong that with a push from her breasts, huge trees got uprooted and the earth split under her feet. She picked up Shukra, stuffed him into her vaginal passage and vanished into space. When Shukra was thus seized, the *daityas* got frightened and started running away from the battlefield. And the army of the *daityas* got scattered.

The *asura* generals like Shumbha, Nishumbha, Kalanemi and others, wild with anger, got their armies together and started fighting with renewed fury. The volley of arrows shot were like swarms of locust which enveloped the entire atmosphere. Streams of blood resembling the *Kimshuka* (Butea monosperma) tree in flower, flowed unabated. The earth shook with all kinds of noises, shouts of joy, leonine roars and with the sound of *damarukas*. The *bhuta-ganas* of Shiva ran, devouring the *danavas*. On seeing his army being destroyed, Jalandhara rushed at the *ganas*. Seeing their leader on the battlefield, the defeated *daityas* got courage and got ready for battle once again. The sound of trumpets, the neighing of horses, the rumbling of chariots and the sound of conches and war-drums rose. The space between heaven and earth was covered so thickly by discharged arrows that it gave the impression of floating masses of mists. And then the battle between Karttikeya and Jalandhara started. Sometimes one was victorius and sometimes the other. Finally, Shiva entered the fray to fight Jalandhara.

Jalandhara aimed a volley of arrows at Shiva and rushed to kill him but Shiva was far more powerful than Jalandhara. When the *daitya* realised the might of Shiva, he created an illusion of *apsaras* and *gandharvas* dancing and singing before Shiva. Shiva got fascinated with the music and dance and Jalandhara urged by lust, entrusted the commands of his army to his generals Shumbha and Nishumbha, and went to visit Parvati. With his demonic powers, he assumed the form of Shiva which had ten arms, five faces, three eyes, matted hair and was seated on a bull. Presuming that he was Shiva, Parvati came forward to meet him. When Jalandhara saw her, he was so enchanted by her beauty that drops of his semen fell and his limbs became numb. Parvati at once realised that he was a demon and vanished to the northern shores of Manasa lake. Defeated in his mission,

Jalandhara went back to fight Shiva.

Parvati was very upset at Jalandhara's audacity. She sent for Vishnu and said to him: "Jalandhara has perpetrated a base deed. Go and violate the chastity of his wife. The *daitya* cannot be killed otherwise."

Vishnu, at the command of Parvati, went to Jalandhara's city to practise deception. Capable of creating illusions, he first took the form of a handsome body. Then assuming the form of an ascetic, he went and sat in a park outside the city, and by his powers made Vrinda, the wife of Jalandhara see a dream. In the dream she saw the naked form of her husband, annointed with oil, seated on a bull and travelling towards the south. His head was shaved and he was wearing black flowers, and there was complete darkness surrounding him. Later in the night, Vrinda had other bad dreams like a city submerged by the sea, the rising sun with a hole in its middle constantly rising and fading. She realised that her dream was ominous and started weeping.

To calm her agitated mind, Vrinda went for a stroll to the park but she did not find any solace there either. Instead she came across demons who had leonine faces and sharp fang-like teeth which frightened her even more. To escape them, she ran breathlessly till she came across the ascetic sitting in the park with a calm countenance. Seeing her frightened face with the demons following her, the sage drove them away with a loud sound, 'Hum'.

Vrinda was struck with wonder at the demons who got terrified and routed by a mere *humkara*. She bowed before the ascetic and said: "O sage, you are omniscient. My husband Jalandhara has gone to fight Shiva. O holy one, tell me how he is."

The ascetic feigned a deceptive silence and looked sympathetic. In the meanwhile, two large monkeys came and stood bowing before him. At a gesture from the ascetic, they rose into the sky and returned bringing the dismembered body of Jalandhara. On seeing her husband's body lying before her in pieces, Vrinda fell unconscious. On regaining consciousness, Vrinda bewailed her husband's death. Then steadying herself and regaining her self-control, she asked the ascetic to resuscitate him.

The deceptive sage first told her that since the *daitya* had been killed by Shiva himself, he could not be brought back to life. But later he agreed to restore his life.

After restoring to life the dismembered body lying before Vrinda, the sage, who was really Vishnu, vanished. The body, an exact replica of Jalandhara, on having been revived, stood up and Vrinda, delighted to see one who she thought was her husband, embraced and kissed him. And the two sported with each other for many days in the forest. One day, at the end of her amorous dalliance with him, she realised that it was Vishnu in the form of Jalandhara and not her real husband. She rebuked him angrily and cursed him,

"O base foe of the *daityas*, defiler of other people's virtue, I curse you. The two persons, whom you made to appear before me, shall, in another life, become *rakshasas* and abduct your wife, thus causing you great distress. You will roam in the forest with Shesha, the lord of snakes who posed as your disciple just now and you will have to depend on the help of monkeys to rescue your wife."

Vrinda's curse came true. Vishnu was born on earth as Ramachandra and when in exile, his wife Sita was abducted by two *rakshasas*, Marichi and Ravana. He was accompanied on his exile by his brother Lakshmana who was an incarnation of the cosmic snake Shesha.

As this drama was being enacted, Jalandhara returned to the battlefield and the deceptive *gandharvas* and *apsaras*, created earlier by him, disappeared. Shiva realised this deception and became furious at Jalandhara's audacity and started shooting arrows at him. Finding Shiva more powerful than him, Jalandhara, in order to delude Shiva again, created an illusion of Parvati harnessed to a chariot, and being harassed by the *daityas*. She was crying bitterly. Seeing his consort in such an abject state and forgetting his own divinity, Shiva became dejected like a mortal and was completely demoralised. Jalandhara at that moment hit Shiva on the head. At this the illusion created by Jalandhara vanished. Shiva, without losing any time assumed a dreadful form which blazed all around, seeing which the *daityas*, including their commanders, fled in terror. At their flight from the battlefield, Shiva rebuked them:

"You wicked rogues", he said, "after offending me and harassing Parvati, you are now deserting the battlefield. Since I do not kill anyone who flees from the battle, you shall be killed by Parvati."

Jalandhara was infuriated by this remark and in revenge hit the bull Nandi with an iron club. Shiva in retaliation put forward an unbearable splendour which was like the fire of dissolution which comes at the end of an age, engulfing all. He also made a wheel by means of his big toe in the waters of the ocean and addressing Jalandhara laughingly said:

"O Jalandhara, if you are powerful enough to lift the wheel created by me, then you will be competent to stand and fight with me, not otherwise."

At this challenge, the eyes of the *Daitya* blazed with anger. He looked angrily at Shiva and said: "After lifting the wheel, I shall kill you and your *ganas*. In the entire three worlds, no one can escape being pierced by my arrow. I defeated Brahma when I was a mere baby. I once burnt the entire universe in a second. Even Indra, Agni, Yama, Kubera, Vayu and Varuna were unable to endure my valour. I have never before been obstructed in my path. Mountains Mandara, Meru and Nila were badly hit by me because I wanted to remove the itching sensation in my arms. Just for sport, I checked the flow of river Ganga. I seized the submarine fire Vadava and closed its mouth and all the oceans became one single unit. I hurled Airavata and other elephants into the ocean. Indra, along with his chariot, was thrown by me to a distance of a hundred *yojanas*. I once even bound Garuda and Vishnu with a serpent and imprisoned many *apsaras*. You have no conception of my strength."

Slighted and insulted by the harsh words of the *Daitya*, Shiva hurled the wheel he had made in the waters at him. The wheel, blazing like a million suns, severed the head of the *Daitya*. His body fell on the earth, making a loud resonant sound and the blood oozing out from his body filled the entire universe. At Shiva's orders, his body and blood were sent to *Maharaurava*, the hell where the souls of the wicked are sent. But since Jalandhara had emanated from Shiva, his soul merged with the soul of Shiva and the splendour coming out of his body merged with the splendour of Shiva. When Jalandhara was killed, the *devatas, gandharvas, naags* and other beings were delighted. They showered flowers at Shiva and sang his glory. The celestial damsels sang and danced with joy, and the wind started blowing gently.

At the death of her husband, Vrinda entered the funeral pyre of her husband and became *sati,* though Vishnu tried his best to prevent her from self-immolation as by that time he had got enamoured of her.

Shiva killed his son Jalandhara as he had become evil. This is a parallel episode of Vishnu killing his son Naraka, born from his wife Bhudevi. Naraka became an evil being and Vishnu in his incarnation as Krishna, killed him.

THE VANISHING OF VISHNU'S ILLUSION

After Vrinda became a *sati,* Vishnu was dejected as he had seriously got infatuated by her charms. He smeared his body with ashes from her funeral pyre and even though advised by *siddhas* and sages, he was inconsolable. Ultimately the *devatas* approached Shiva and asked him to make Vishnu see sense. To this Shiva replied:

"My Maya deluded all and it cannot be transgressed. The entire universe is subservient to me. Vishnu too was deluded by that illusion and became a prey to lust and love. That illusion has various names. It is Uma, Mahadevi, the three mothers Amba, Ambika, Ambalika, the three sisters who represent the three fires of the cosmic *yajna,* the three mothers who create the three great principles of mind, life and matter. It is the greatest primordial *Mulaprakrti* called Parvati. Seek refuge in her for the removal of Vishnu's delusion. She concedes the desires of her devotees. Sing her praise and if she, my Shakti, is satisfied, she will carry out your task."

The gods then eulogised the primordial *Prakriti* who is favourably disposed towards her devotees. "We bow to the

primordial *Prakriti"*, they said, "from whom emanate the
three attributes *rajas sattva,* and *tamas* that are the cause
of creation, sustenance and annihilation and by whose wishes
the universe is evolved and dissolved. O magnificent
Goddess, you alone can remove the delusion of Vishnu."

Just then a celestial voice was heard from the heavens
saying: "O Gods, it is indeed I, who am the three forms
representing the three attributes *rajas, sattva* and *tamas.*
The three forms are the three goddesses Saraswati, Lakshmi
and Gauri. Hence, you should go to them and eulogise them.
If they are pleased with you, then they will fulfil every desire
of yours."

The gods went and placed their petition before the
goddesses Saraswati, Lakshmi and Gauri. The three
goddesses gave some seeds to the gods and said:

"Sow these seeds in the place where Vishnu is standing
in a trance, enchanted by Vrinda, and then your wishes will
be realised."

Saying this, the goddesses who were the female energies
of Brahma, Vishnu and Shiva, vanished. The gods sowed
the seeds given to them at the place where the pyre of Vrinda
was lit and where Vishnu was standing as if in a trance.
Out of the seeds sown, three plants came out. They were
Dhatri Jasmine and *Tulasi. Dhatri* was born of Brahma's
Shakti Saraswati, *Tulasi,* of Vishnu's Shakti called Lakshmi
and *Jasmine* of Gauri who was Shiva's *Shakti.* They were
born of the three attributes, *rajas sattva* and *tamas*
respectively. On seeing the plants in the form of ladies,
Vishnu got excited and forgot his infatuation with Vrinda.
The two plants, *Tulasi* and *Dhatri,* looked at him lovingly
but the woman-like plant born out of the *Shakti* of Shiva,
became jealous of Vrinda and hence came to be called *Varvari*
and was despised by all. It is also called *Malati* or Barbari
(Jasminium grandiflorum) and is forbidden in the worship
of Vishnu. But the other two plants Dhatri (Embelica
officinalis) and *Tulasi* (Ocimum sanctum) were pleasing to
Vishnu because of their love and affection for him.

The task of the gods was accomplished. Vishnu forgot
all his sorrow and accompanied by the three ladies went
back to Vaikuntha. *Dhatri* and *Tulasi* are the favourites of

the gods and are offered to them especially in the month
of *Kartika*. They are offered to all the gods except Ganesha.

KALI BECOMES GAURI

Parvati saw a handsome youth called Viraka (same as
Skanda) and wished to have a son like him. Parvati adopted
him as her son at the suggestion of Shiva. Soon after this,
Parvati was touched by night and she became black in colour.
Seeing her complexion turned black, Shiva found fault with
her and called her *Kali* or *Shyama*. Parvati was hurt at
Shiva calling her Kali and left him to do penance. Her
adopted son Viraka, who was deeply attached to her, begged
her not to go but she insisted and said that she had been
gravely insulted by Shiva and would only return as Gauri,
the fair-complexioned one. She asked Viraka to guard her
apartments and not let any woman enter them in her
absence. During her absence, Adi, the son of Andhakasura,
entered the apartments of Shiva in the guise of a snake and
after getting into her apartments, he assumed the form of
Uma, the consort of Shiva. Because of a boon given to him
by Brahma, he could change his form only twice and the
second change was to be followed by his death. Shiva
discovered his form and identity when Adi changed his form
one after another and killed him as he assumed the form
of Uma, (Parvati).

When Uma, after having become the fair-complexioned
Gauri, entered the apartments of Shiva, she was stopped at
the gate by Viraka who did not recognise her at first. The
story of Adi in the form of a woman in the apartments of
Shiva had reached Gauri. She cursed Viraka to be born
on earth for letting a woman enter Shiva's bedroom. Her
anger at Viraka was so great that out of her rage, a lion
arose. This lion was given to the goddess of night by Brahma.

BIRTH OF ANDHAKA

Once Shiva, accompanied by Parvati and his *ganas*, went
to Kashi and after appointing Bhairava, a fearful aspect of
himself which haunts the cremation-grounds, as the protector
of the city, he returned to Mount Mandara. During his stay

SHIVA

76

on the eastern ridges of the mountain, Parvati sportively
put her hands on Shiva's eyes. With Shiva's eyes closed,
darkness spread all around. The contact of her hands with
his eyes brought perspiration. This perspiration was very
hot because of the fire coming out of Shiva's third eye. From
this perspiration, a terrifying looking creature, was born.
This creature had a bad temper, was ungrateful, blind,
deformed and was black in colour. He had matted locks,
and hair grew all over his body. He behaved like a mad
man by sometimes singing, crying, laughing or dancing and
stuck out his tongue like a serpent and thundered like a
cloud. Seeing him, Parvati got frightened. Shiva smiled
at her and said:

"You are responsible for this creation. Why are you now
afraid of it?"

Hearing Shiva's words, Parvati removed her hands from
his eyes and light spread all around. In the bright light,
the blind creature appeared even more terrible. Seeing this
strange being, Parvati asked Shiva: "Who is this ugly being?
Whose child is he and why was he created?"

Shiva replied: "When you closed my eyes, this being was
born out of the perspiration formed by contact with your
hands. Since he is blind, I will name him Andhaka. And
now his well-being rests with you. I request you to welcome
him as your son and to look after him. I will order my
ganas to guard him."

About this time, *daitya* Hiranyaksha desired a son.
Actually he was being pressed for a son by his wife who
was envious at the many sons her husband's brother
Hiranyakashipu had. To realise his wishes, Hiranyaksha
repaired to a forest and performed many penances. Shiva,
pleased with his penance, appeared before him and agreed
to grant him the boon of a son but said:

"O ruler of the *daityas*, there will not be a son born
to you, but I shall grant you a son. My son Andhaka has
powers equal to yours and he cannot be defeated by anyone.
Accept him as your son and stop your penance."

The *Daitya* circumbulated Shiva, worshipped him, sang
hymns of praise and happily returned to his kingdom with
his adopted son. Hiranyaksha by his austerities became very

powerful, conquered all the gods and even dragged the earth to *Patala,* the subterranean region. He forgot his earlier pious life and started inflicting atrocities on all. As the atrocities perpetuated by Hiranyaksha became unendurable, the celestials, *siddhas* and sages propitiated Vishnu in his incarnation as a Boar, a form that constitutes all the sacrifices. Vishnu as Varaha the Boar, split the earth by beating and striking with his snout and entered *Patala.* He crushed hundreds of *daityas* with his nose and with his fangs, smashed the armies of the *asuras* by merely kicking with his legs, cut off Hiranyaksha's head with his *sudarshana-chakra* and reduced him to ashes. After killing Hiranyaksha, he crowned his adopted son Andhaka as the king of the *daityas.*

Varaha then lifted the Earth with his fangs and restored her to her original place and returned to his abode.

When Hiranyakashipu heard about the death of his elder brother Hiranyaksha, he decided to avenge his death. To become invincible, unaging, unrivalled in strength, he performed a severe penance in the ravines of the Mandara mountain. The smoke from the fire of his penance which sprang from his head, spread all around and scorched the world on all sides. The gods scorched by the fire abandoned heaven and went to Brahma's *Satyaloka* and informed the Creator of what was happening. On hearing their tale of woe, Brahma accompanied by holy sages like Bhrigu and Daksha, went to the *Daitya* and offered him a boon if he would stop his penance. Hiranyakashipu agreed to the pact and asked for the following boon:

"Let there be no death for me in heaven or on earth, in the day time or at night, from above or from below, inside the house or outside and let me be invincible to god, man and animal."

Brahma replied: "Stop your penance. It has already run into 96,000 years. Your desires are granted."

Once Hiranyakashipu was coronated by Brahma and given the boon of near invincibiliy, he became arrogant. He started disturbing all righteous activities and even defeated the gods in battle. The terrified celestials approached Vishnu for a redress of their grivances. Because of Brahma's boon

to him, it was not an easy task to destroy Hiranyakashipu.
And yet to get-rid of him was essential. So to help the
celestials, Vishnu took the form of Narasimha, half-man,
half-lion, and came out of a pillar which was neither inside
nor outside, at dusk which was neither day nor night and
killed Hiranyakashipu.

Narasimha incarnation of Vishnu became very arrogant
for having accomplished what was considered almost an
impossibility. To curb his arrogance, Shiva ripped off the
skin of the lion with his nail and wrapped it round his body.
And that is why Shiva wears the lion skin.

When Hiranyakashipu was killed, cousins of Andhaka
taunted him and said: "O blind fellow, what will you do with
a kingdom? Hiranyaksha was a fool to have adopted a blind
son. You are also ugly and hideous to look at and fond
of quarrelling. Only a real son of a king can lay claim
to the throne. How can you aspire to it?"

Andhaka felt unhappy at these words of his cousins and
went away to the forest to practise austerities. He cut off
a piece of his flesh daily and consigned it to the sacred fire
as an offering till only his bones were left which also he
finally decided to sacrifice. At his severe penance, the
heaven dwellers got frightened. Panicking at this
superhuman sacrifice, they propitiated Brahma and asked
him to intervene and stop the sacrifice. Brahma visited
Andhaka at the request of the gods and offered him a boon
if he would desist from further sacrifice.

Andhaka answered: "Let the *daityas* who have usurped
my kingdom, be my slaves. Even though I was born blind,
let me be endowed with divine vision. Let no death come
to me from celestials, *daityas, gandharvas, yakshas, naags,*
humans, Vishnu or even from Shiva."

At this request, Brahma got suspicious and said: "O
Daitya, whatever you ask, you will get. But accept some
cause of death because none who is born or will be born
can escape the jaws of death. Actually good men like you
should avoid too long a life."

Andhaka answered: "If that is so, then let death befall
me if I ever covert the most excellent of ladies, of whatever
age, however beautiful and unapproachable she may be even

in the three worlds, if such a woman is like a mother to me."

Brahma was surprised at such a request but agreed to the boon that Andhaka had asked for. He then touched Andhaka with his hands and the latter's sight was restored to him and from a mere skin and bones, he became a full-bodied, handsome man.

When Andhaka entered his city after the restoration of his sight and looks, there was an aura of divinity surrounding him and Prahlada and other *daityas* realised that he was blessed with a boon. They became his slaves and surrendered their entire kingdom to him. Andhaka defeated Indra and made him pay tribute to him. He conquered the *naags, suparnas, rakshasas, gandharvas, yakshas,* human beings and animals. He made the animate and the inanimate world subservient to him. He passed 10,000 years sporting with thousands of women whom he had forcibly taken and in drinking intoxicating beverages.

Blinded by pride and arrogance, he started associating with the wicked. He destroyed *Vedic* rites and attacked scholars so that learning of scriptures suffered. Proud of his affluence, he slighted the *Vedas,* gods and preceptors and thus continued to live for millions of years. During this time, he was travelling all over the universe and, in his wanderings, chanced to go into the valleys of the Mandara mountain. Seeing a beautiful spot, he decided to stay there. One day, during his stay in the valley of the Mandara mountain, his ministers Duryodhana, Vaidhasa and Hasti, saw a beautiful woman and hastened to tell Andhaka about it.

"O Lord, we have seen in a mountain cavern, a sage with his eyes closed and in deep meditation. He has a handsome face with the crescent moon adorning his head and an elephant hide round his hips. Serpents twine round his body, a necklace of skulls round his neck and he has matted hair. He holds a trident in one hand and a rosary in the other and also has arrows and quiver. He wields a sword and this fair-complexioned, four-armed sage, even with his body smeared with ashes, shines with a dazzling splendour. The guard on duty near him also has similar

features but with a terrible expression. There is also a
woman besides this sage and she has very auspicious
features. She is young and beautiful and is adorned with
precious jewels. This woman is a rare gem under the sun.
O *Daitya*, this divine lady, the wife of the sage, should be
brought here. You deserve her more than the ascetic does."

On hearing these words of his generals, *Daitya* Andhaka
shook with excitement and lustful thoughts. He decided that
the beautiful lady mentioned should become his wife. With
this in mind, he sent his messenger Duryodhana to Shiva.

Duryodhana approached Shiva and said: "Andhaka, the
Emperor of three worlds is camping in the ravines of the
Mandara mountain. He wants to know whose son you are
and why you are living here and whose wife is this young
and beautiful woman. She must be given to him. Why
is your body smeared with ashes and decorated with
necklaces of skulls and bones? Why do you keep the quiver,
the sword, the missile *Bhushundi*, the trident, the
thunderbolt and the iron club? Why do you have the sacred
Ganga, the crescent moon, matted hair, bones and skulls
poisonous serpents and at the same time this lady of plump
bosom? Surrender your wife peacefully to me. It is not proper
to do penance in the company of a lady. Leave off your
weapons and carry on your penance. If you transgress my
orders, you will have to pay for it with your life."

Shiva listened to this tirade with perfect composure.
When Andhaka's emissary had finished talking, he calmly
answered him: "I do not remember my parents. I am
performing a fast and the *Pashupata* rite in this cavern, the
like of which has not yet been performed. It is true that
I have no roots but still my young and beautiful wife bears
patiently with me. She was acquired as a result of pious
deeds performed by me in the past. As far as my weapons
are concerned, I cannot get rid of them as they are a part
of me. O *Daitya*, tell your master, he can try and take
what appeals to him."

Duryodhana bowed to Shiva and returned to Andhaka
with Shiva's reply, adding: "O king, you are the Emperor
of the *daityas* and yet you have been mocked disparagingly
by a pitiable penance monger. He considers the three worlds

of no significance."

Saying this, Andhaka's generals incited him further and encouraged him to fight Shiva by saying: "No *Nishachara* (night-walker) lacks in heroism and courage. A *danava* is not powerless, nor is he ruthless, ungrateful, sinful or afraid of death."

After Andhaka's emissary left Shiva, jackals began to howl and dance amidst putrifying fat and flesh and beasts of prey, ghosts and spirits began to roam around. Parvati was frightened at seeing them but Shiva consoled her by saying: "Beloved, formerly I had performed a *vrata* called *Mahapashuspata*. But the strength that I had derived from it is now exhausted. That is why the immortals have had to suffer at the hands of mortals. O Goddess, merit has declined due to my physical contact with you. I will now create a divine forest and shall perform a still more severe *vrata* whereby, you shall be free from fear and sorrow."

Shiva went away to the celestial forest and performed penance there for one thousand years. The performance of this penance required a complete concentration of mind. Hence Parvati was kept away from the scene of his penance in a cave of the Mandara mountain under the care and protection of her son Viraka. Though she was guarded by her son, Parvati was still terrified and unhappy.

Andhaka, deluded and smitten by the arrows of Kamadeva, the god of love, drank wine and accompanied by his soldiers, started from his palace. Like an elephant in rut, he walked towards the cavern and saw Viraka standing firmly and guarding the entrance to the cave. Andhaka went towards the cavern eagerly, almost like a moth approaching a flame. When Viraka questioned him about his identity, he did not reply but instead started fighting with Viraka. It was not difficult for Viraka to defeat Andhaka. Grieved and divested of his pride at his defeat, Andhaka and his followers left the battlefield but Andhaka, smitten by pangs of love, was still not prepared to give up the fight. He reorganised his army and once again attacked. For five hundred and five days and nights, the *Daitya* fought with Viraka. Various weapons were used by the *daityas* and Viraka attacked by them, fainted at the mouth of the cavern. Viraka's body got covered with the weapons hurled at him and the mouth of the cavern got blocked. When Viraka's body could not be extricated, Parvati got frightened and remembered Brahma, Vishnu, Indra and other gods. Thus remembered, the gods came to the rescue of Parvati.

The female energies of the gods produced thunder-like sounds by beating drums and blowing conches. Viraka had also regained consciousness in the meanwhile and started fighting the *daityas* once again.

Brahmni, the female power of Brahma, opposed the *daityas* with her staff; Gauri by her temper; Narayani held the conch, mace, sword, Discus and bow in her hands. Bidaujasi of the golden complexion, with the sky forming her forelocks, set out holding the thunderbolt and the handle of the ploughshare in her hands; the goddess with a thousand eyes fought undaunted. Yamya looked fierce with a staff in her hands and the goddess of fire was not too gentle of face either. Nairrti held a fierce bow and a sharp sword. The female form Varuni held a noose in her hands to fight while the female form of the storm gods took hunger for her physical body and held the goad in her hands. The female energy of Kubera, the Yaksha lord, blazing like fire, held a mace in her hands. She was sharp-faced with a hideous look. The female form of the Naags had claws for her weapons. All these and other goddesses set forth to fight the *daityas*. The female energies of the gods were limitless in number and seeing them the *daityas* were frightened and at the same time dejected.

Brahma's Shakti was the chief of the celestial damsels. Viraka pacified the mind of Parvati. Parvati made Viraka the general of her army and herself entered the battlefield to fight the *daityas*. Andhaka made Gila the general of his army and started fighting to capture Parvati. Infuriated at the audacity of Andhaka, Shiva, shining with the lustre of a thousand suns, himself came and joined the fight against Andhaka. He embraced Parvati and the two went inside the cave. Andhaka could not bear to see the two together and sent his messenger Vighasa to speak to Shiva. The messenger addressing Shiva said:

"I have been sent by my lord Andhaka. He says that

you are an ascetic and should, therefore, have nothing to do with a woman. Surrender this young and beautiful woman to me or else I challenge you to a fight and can assure you, O wicked ascetic, that I shall send you to Yama's abode."

Shiva naturally was furious at these words of the messenger and replied: "Let the haughty *Daitya*, proud of his strength, come and fight with me."

Andhaka, on getting Shiva's reply, attacked the cavern with his army. Shiva also retaliated and sent his army to the mouth of the cave. But the *Daitya* proved to be the stronger of the two, and in no time, Brahma, Vishnu, Indra, Surya, Chandrama, Yama, Varuna, Vayu, Kubera and their armies were swallowed by Vighasa. Only Viraka was left. He rushed to Shiva to inform him of what had happened.

This plight of Vishnu was due to a curse. Vishnu in his incarnation as Narasimha had the speed of wind and a terrifying demeanour. After tearing Hiranyakashipu with his claws and thus killing him, a feat that was considered an impossibility, he had become haughty and had started blowing off the three worlds with his mouth. Annoyed at this, the rishis cursed him and said: "You will be crushed by the *daityas* and remain defeated for a long time."

Vishnu asked: "When will I get rid of this curse, O rishis?" The rishis replied: "During the battle with the *daityas*, you will be swallowed by Vighasa. Later you will be freed by Shiva in a cave of the Badari forest. (Jujabe mauritiana)"

As this curse was pronounced by the sages, Shiva curbed Vishnu's arrogance by ripping off his tiger skin with his nail and wrapping it round his body.

When Viraka narrated to Shiva how Vighasa was swallowing the *ganas* and how Shukra, the preceptor of the *daityas*, was reviving their dead killed in battle, Shiva recited the *Samaveda*, then laughed and assumed a body resplendent as the sun. And thus darkness which had enveloped the universe was dispelled. When light appeared, Viraka again started fighting with the *daityas* and this time, Nandin and he were both swallowed by Vighasa. Seeing this, Shiva, riding his bull, faced the *Daitya* Vighasa and repeated the divine *mantra* which disgorges what has been swallowed. At

this all those who were swallowed by Vighasa came tumbling
out of his body and started fighting the *daityas*. But Shukra
continued to revive the dead *daityas*. In desperation, Shiva's
ganas, bound Shukra and brought him before Shiva. To stop
the *daityas* from being revived, Shiva swallowed Shukra.

When Shukra was no more, the *danavas* were destroyed.
The battle ground was soon full of *bhutas* devouring the
corpses of the *daityas* and with *Vetalas*, vultures, jackals and
dancing bodies. What was left of the exhausted army of
the *daityas* entered the nether regions and filled every nook
and corner, but Andhaka, even with his body shattered by
weapons and missiles, did not leave off fighting as he had
a boon by which not even a god could kill him.

Many Andhakas, resembling the *Daitya* Andhaka, arose
from the exudation out of the body of the *Daitya*. Shiva
pierced him with his trident but armies of Andhakas cropped
up from every drop of his blood that fell. Iconographically,
sometimes Shiva is depicted as fighting Andhakasura with
one hand and carrying a bowl in the other hand to collect
the drops of blood that fell from the *asura's* wounds.

Vishnu with his *yogic* knowledge assumed the form of
a hideous-looking woman, who had several arms and stood
in the battlefield covering the entire space by her two feet.
She was eulogised by the gods and then this hungry female
devoured the army and drank the blood of the *daityas* till
the battle ground became marshy and only the chief of the
daityas was left alive. Although the blood of Andhaka was
sucked dry, he still fought with Shiva. Shiva pierced his
heart and staked him on his trident and held him hanging
in the sky. The lower half of his body got dried by the
strong rays of the sun and the upper half was drenched by
the clouds. The *Daitya* did not die even though he was
tortured in many ways and his legs were torn asunder. When
he could no longer suffer the tortures, he eulogised Shiva
and begged his pardon. Shiva was delighted at this change
of heart and not only forgave him but also made him the
chief of his *ganas*.

Andhaka personifies ego, arrogance and darkness.
Symbolically, it is the darkness of the mind which is due
to the arrogant nature of man which blinds him to the

presence of the Supreme Soul and Shiva destroys not
Andhaka but the arrogance in him.

When Vishnu in his incarnation as Narasimha killed
Hiranyakasipu, he became very arrogant. To curb that
arrogance, Shiva manifested himself as Sharabha, a mythical
being, part beast, part bird with sharp claws and eight feet.
Seeing him Narasimha, the man-lion, beat him with his tail.
Sharabha retaliated and beat him with his wings and pecked
at him with his adamantine claws. Finally faint with dread,
Narasimha surrenderd. Sharabha killed him, and stripped
his lion hide and presented it to Shiva, who wore it on
his body and came to be called *Krittivasa*.

BHASMASURA, THE DEMON OF ASHES

Vrikasura was a devotee of Shiva. Pleased with his
austerities and devotion to him, Shiva granted him the boon
of turning to ashes anyone on whose head he placed his hand.
To test the efficacy of this boon, Vrikasura in his arrogance
tried to put his hands on Shiva. To save Shiva from
Vrikasura, Vishnu took the from of the beautiful seductress
Mohini and started dancing with him. Enamoured of Mohini,
Vrikasura tried to keep pace with her and copied all the
mudras that Mohini attempted. Mohini while dancing put
her hands on her own head. Vrikasura followed her gestures
and put his hands on his own head and was turned to ashes.
Since then he came to be known as Bhasmasura, the demon
of ashes.

6

PARVATI ACCEPTS SHUKRA AS SON

When Shukra was swallowed by Shiva, the *daityas* were demoralised as there was no one left who could revive their dead.

Andhaka addressed his followers and said: "By seizing Bhargava Shukra from our midst, we have been rendered lifeless. Our courage, valour, fame, strength, splendour and exploits are of no use. Shame on us that we could not protect our preceptor. Let us not waste any more time. We must start fighting the enemy at once. I shall slay the *Pramathas* along with Nandin and save Shukra. If we are destined to survive, then no one can destroy us."

The armies of the *Pramathas* and of the *daityas* made a tumultuous noise. Hearing this noise, Shukra who was within the belly of Shiva, began to wander about, looking for an outlet. In Shiva's body, he observed the seven worlds, the different worlds of Brahma, Vishnu, Indra, Aditya, the celestial damsels as well as the battle between the *Pramathas* and the *daityas*. But wandering in the belly of Shiva even for hundreds of years, he did not find a way out. Finally, he resorted to *Yoga* of Shiva, repeated a special *mantra*, and assuming the form of Shiva's semen, emerged out of his body through his penis. He bowed to Shiva and Parvati accepted him as her son. Shiva made him the chief of some of his *ganas*, named him Shukra and made him unaging and immortal.

Shukra, known for his deep understanding and knowledge of the *Vedas,* was reborn as a son of Shiva, when the earth was three thousand years old.

THE STORY OF SHITALA MANGALA

Once a prince offered a sacrifice to the gods to obtain a son. From the dying embers of the sacrificial fire, a beautiful maiden was created. Brahma, the presiding deity of the ceremony who conducted the sacrifice, named her Shitala, which means the cooling one. On coming into existence, Shitala asked Brahma 'about the powers she possessed. Brahma assured her that she would always be worshipped by the mortals if she took some lentils as it would be the power of the lentils that would make her worshipful to them. Shitala next asked for a companion. Brahma directed her to Shiva saying that he would provide her with a companion. Shitala visited the celestial spheres where Shiva was in eternal meditation. Eulogised by her, Shiva agreed to give her a companion. From the drops of sweat which fell due to his powers of asceticism, a demon was born. The demon was so enormous that Shiva had to cut him into three pieces. Brahma, however, restored the body of the demon. But now the demon had three sets of arms and legs. He was named Jvarasur, which literally means the fever-demon, and Shiva assigned him to Shitala as a companion.

Shitala required a beast of burden to carry her heavy bag of lentils and her companion Jvarasur suggested that she take an ass. Shitala and Jvarasur disguised themselves as an old woman and a boy respectively, and with their bag of lentils on the back of an ass, visited all the celestials in the heavenly sphere. Somehow, the lentils got converted miraculously into pox germs and the gods were afflicted with fever and small-pox. Thus afflicted, the celestials begged mercy and promised to worship Shitala on condition that she would go with her bag of lentils to the earth.

Shitala agreed and proceeded to the earth. On earth, to prove her powers over men, she first visited King Virata who was an ardent devoteed of Shiva. Virat accepted her as a goddess but refused to give her precedence over Shiva. Shitala threatened him with her powers of inflicting small-pox but in spite of all her threats, he refused to give in to her. To humble him, Shitala called together a host of dread diseases and seventyfive different types of poxes. Each one of them boasted of the misery it could inflict on those who refused to worship Shitala. Even then King Virata would not allow his people to worship her, as a result of which epidemics spread and death was the outcome. Those who finally acknowledged her supremacy including King Virata, were miraculously restored to their normal health.

Shitala is described as a beautiful woman dressed in a yellow saree, which is the colour of spring. Since she visits homes in spring she is called Vasanta, i.e., spring. She is often accompanied by a maid called Raktavati, who has power over the illness called measles. Shitala has a winnowing fan above her head and holds a silver broom in one hand and a golden water pot in the other. Shitala's broom, it is said, sweeps away those who do not worship her. The pox germs are stored in her waterpot and sifted by her winnowing fan. She hates dirt and, therefore, while she is visiting a household which means that someone is afflicted by the pox illness, it has to be sprinkled with the waters of river Ganga. Ganga is the personified wife of Shiva. *Neem (Azadirachta indica)* or banana (*Musa paradisica*) leaves are freshly laid under or in the bed as well as on the floor of the sick room. Incense and camphor are burnt twice a day to disinfect the house and *neem* leaves hung on the door to announce her presence in the house. Shitala is one of seven sisters and her presence means that the disease called small-pox has arrived. Incidence of small-pox is referred to as mother's kindness (*Mai daya*) or mother's play (*Mai khela*) and never derogatively lest she strike the victim dead.

PARVATI IS BORN AS A FISHERWOMAN

Parvati had undergone severe austerities and penances to win Shiva as her husband. But on getting married she found that he was a Mahayogi who was only interested in philosophical discussions and in giving discourses on subjects that were of no interest to her. It so happened that one day, while Shiva was explaining some obstruse philosophical point to her, Parvati, out of boredom, fell asleep. Shiva looked up and, finding Parvati's head drooping with sleep, rebuked her for being inattentive. Thus caught red-handed, Parvati tried to justify her closed eyes and nodding head by saying that she was not asleep but had closed her eyes only to concentrate better on what he was saying. To test her statement, Shiva asked her to repeat what he had said earlier. Parvati could not do so and Shiva angry at his wife, cursed her to become a fisher-woman on earth. And almost instantaneously on being cursed, Parvati fell down to earth in a fishermen's colony as a beautiful baby girl.

After the departure of his wife, Shiva tried to forget her and assuming his characteristic pose of a *yogi*, tried to meditate. But he was so much in love with Parvati that he found it impossible to concentrate. Thoughts of Parvati tormented him day and night. When he could no longer endure her absence, he thought that it was better to get her back than to suffer the pangs of separation. But to get her back from among the fisherfolk was no easy matter. The tactics had to be arranged with great dignity. Shiva thought of a ruse. He asked his *gana* Nandi to take the form of a shark and to break the nets of the fishermen who had given shelter to Parvati.

On falling to earth from Mount Kailash, Parvati had been picked up by the Chief of the fisherfolk who adopted her and brought her up as his own daughter. As the fisherman's adopted daughter grew up, her beauty increased with every passing day and all the young fishermen wished to have her as their wife. About the same time, Nandi, in the form of a shark, was creating havoc and destroying the nets of all fishermen. The fishermen tried their best to catch the shark, but failed. When the situation became desperate, the Chief of fishermen declared that he would give his beautiful daughter in marriage to one who would catch the shark. Shiva was waiting for just such an opportunity. Assuming the form of a fisherman, he contested with the others and as was to be expected, he easily caught the shark. The Chief of the fishermen, true to his word, married his daughter to him. Shiva then assumed his natural form and left with Parvati for his abode on Mount Kailash.

SHIVA FALLS IN LOVE WITH A DOM GIRL

When the earth was created, the *daityas* also made their appearance. They were strong and arrogant. Vishnu decided to curb their arrogance. It was not a difficult task for him and in no time they were annihilated. When the *daityas* were defeated, the gods and other celestials celebrated their victory by having a feast. They requested Shiva to ask Ganga, the wife of Shantanu, to cook a meal to be served to the victorius. Shiva went to Shantanu and asked for the loan of his wife Ganga. Shantanu agreed to let his wife go with Shiva to cook the meal but on the understanding that she must return by nightfall, otherwise he would not accept her back. But the food took a long time to cook and the feast lasted till very late at night. When Ganga returned to Shantanu in the early hours of the morning, he refused to accept her back and she had to return to Shiva, and he accepted her as his wife.

Shiva started austere penances on the banks of the river Balluka in order to obtain a sight of Dharma. His austerities continued for twelve long years. Once when Shiva was not in his hermitage, Dharma, riding an owl and with a white umbrella over his head, visited his house. Ganga came out of the house to receive him and instantly her dress and complexion turned white. Dharma asked Ganga to inform Shiva of his visit. Ganga requested him to pay another visit so that Shiva could also meet him. Dharma replied that the same merit would be attained by Shiva when he looked at her and added that if Shiva was not satisfied with that, he ought to go and pluck flowers at Kalidaha where he would see him in the form of a celestial damsel.

Shiva on return to the hermitage was surprised to see Ganga all white. He lamented having missed the opportunity of meeting Dharma. The news of Dharma's visit to Shiva's house spread all around, and gods and goddesses came to see Ganga who now radiated a divine light for having seen Dharma in person.

Abiding by Dharma's instructions, Shiva went to Kalidaha to pluck flowers. One day his wife Gauri, curious to know why he went daily to Kalidaha, expressed a wish to accompany him. But Shiva restrained her from accompanying him and said that the lake was full of poisonous snakes. Gauri agreed to stay back but being full of curiosity, she could not restrain herself. Disguising herself as a beautiful Dom girl, she followed him and took the place of a ferry girl on the river Joka which had to be crossed to go to Kalidaha. Shiva hired her to ferry him across the river. The Dom girl was very beautiful and Shiva fell in love with her. When he made advances to her, she reminded him that she was a woman of low origin but Shiva was so infatuated with her that he insisted on seducing her and even tried to bribe her by offering her a piece of jewellry. The Dom girl agreed to his proposal and had physical relations with him. Later, the Dom girl revealed her true identity and Gauri, his wife, nagged him for his licentious nature. Thus humiliated, Shiva decided to take revenge. He took the form of a mouse and chewed her blouse. Later he appeared in the guise of a tailor and she engaged him to darn her blouse, promising to pay him well. When the work was done, the tailor refused all material payment and insisted on having physical relations with her in lieu of the money due to him, Gauri had no choice but to agree. Afterwards Shiva threw off his guise and berated her as she herself had once nagged him.

Many days passed after the above incident. Shiva saw birds mating at Kalidaha and got excited, with the consequence that his semen came out which he cast on a lotus leaf. This semen was eaten by a crow but the crow was unable to retain it. Taking the advice of his wife, the crow disgorged it on the same lotus leaf from where he had taken it. From the leaf, the semen travelled down the stalk and finally reached *patala*, the region of Vasuki the serpent, and fell like a thunderbolt on his head. Vasuki's mother was a Naag sculptress. Because of her deep intuitive nature, she immediately realised that the semen was of Shiva. Being a sculptress, she fashioned an image of a beautiful girl and touched that image with his semen. The image coming in contact with the semen became alive. She named the girl Manasa. Manasa grew up to be the goddess of snakes.

Manasa, after coming to life was presented to Vasuki by his mother and he accepted her as his sister. Manasa was given charge of all the poison that was produced when King Prithu milked the earth as a cow. Manasa took her abode in the lake Kalidaha and because of the poison, all the flowers of the lake died. When Shiva was thus deprived of flowers for his worship, he ordered Garuda, the hereditary enemy of snakes, to rid the lake of snakes so that flowers would again grow at Kalidaha. The snake Kali reported the attack of Garuda to Manasa, and Manasa appeared before Shiva to implore him not to kill the snakes. Manasa as a *naag* girl was very beautiful and Shiva fell in love with her. Manasa got frightened at his advances and told him the story of her birth and the fact that she was his daughter.

Manasa wanted to accompany her father to his house but Shiva was afraid of his wife Gauri. But he gave in to her repeated requests and took her home concealed in a flower-basket. Gauri found her in the basket hidden among the flowers and in spite of protests from Manasa suspected her of being a mistress of Shiva. Gauri continued to be suspicious even after Manasa had told her the circumstances under which she was born and after she had affectionately addressed Gauri as mother. This made Manasa lose her temper and she answered Gauri's probings about her background in an arrogant manner. Matters became worse and in anger Gauri jabbed a needle of Kusha grass (Desmostachya bipinnata) in Manasa's eye. Manasa took her revenge on Gauri and looked so ferociously at her with her other eye that Gauri became unconscious. When Shiva was informed of this by his sons Ganesha and Karttikeya, he went to Manasa and requested her to revive Gauri. This incident was not an isolated one but was followed by other quarrels between the two women. Finally, Gauri gave an ultimatum to Shiva and said that she would not live any longer in the same house with Manasa. Shiva decided to look for another abode for Manasa. Before Manasa left, she gave Gauri a signet ring which had five precious gems studded in it and told her to call her immediately if Shiva was ever in danger.

Shiva and Manasa walked many miles looking for a fit

abode for Manasa. Getting tired, they rested on the Sijuya
hill which was covered with *sij* trees (Euphorbia nuvalia)
and Manasa who was very tired fell asleep under a tree.
Seeing her fall asleep, Shiva decided to leave her. At
thoughts of abandoing his daughter, tears fell from Shiva's
eyes. These tears coalesced into a girl who was named Neto.
Neto requested Shiva to stay back but he did not agree and instead
asked her to stay as an attendant of Manasa and look after her
and then left. He had not gone far when he realised that it
was not proper to leave the two girls alone. This thought brought
on sweat on his forehead and from his sweat he created
Dhamai whom he instructed to guard both Manasa and Neto.

Manasa decided to stay on the Sijuya hill and commanded
Vishvakarman, the celestial architect, to build her a palace
there.

The association of snakes with the worship of Shiva is
very old. Shesha, the divine snake, is a son of Shiva. Shiva is
iconographically described as wearing garlands of snakes and also
profusely ornamented with them.

Shesha forms the axle of Shiva's chariot. Snakes
Erapatra and Pushpadanta its modeani; snake Tarksaka the
rope and Vasuki, the string of the bow. *Naags* are shown
on either side of a *lingam* and are usually depicted as
worshipping it. Shiva is sometimes also worshipped as a
coiled cobra. There are *Naag-kuans* or snake wells and pits
where an image of Shiva in the form of a *Lingam* is
worshipped, with snakes carved all around it. Iconographically, Shiva is shown as wearing a girdle, earrings, armlets,
wrist-bands and other ornaments made of snakes. A snake
entwines round his matted hair. His garments and *Upavita*
cord is also formed of snakes. Snakes are in fact connected
with every aspect of the cult of Shiva.

Snakes being symbols of fertility, Manasa is mainly
worshipped as a fertility goddess. She is believed to cure
diseases like cholera and small-pox. She is very popular
as a *Gramdevi* (village goddess) and is said to fulfil the
desires of her devotee, looks after his family and protects
his children. As a tutelary goddess, she provides rain and
wealth.

SHIVA IS ENAMOURED OF MOHINI

The gods in Hindu mythology have human feelings. Like the humans, they get married and have children but being divine, they are endowed with supernatural powers and often the birth of their vast progeny is linked with myths and legends and Shiva, the Supreme Soul, is no exception.

Once when the *daityas* had become very powerful and were ruling the three worlds, the *devatas*, unhappy at being subdued by their enemies, went to Vishnu and complained of the illtreatment metted out to them by the *daityas*. Vishnu promised to redress their grivances. He asked them to churn the ocean of milk after having put all the medicinal herbs into it. As a result of the churning, *amrita*, the drink of immortality that would come out, was to be drunk by them, so that they would become strong and defeat the *daityas*.

As advised by Vishnu, the *devatas* churned the ocean of milk by using mount Mandara as the churning rod and the celestial snake Vasuki as the churning rope. But since Mount Mandara was too heavy for the *devatas* to uproot by themselves, on Vishnu's advice, they asked the *daityas* to help them on the understanding that the ambrosia churned out of the ocean would be equally shared by all of them. Vishnu himself in the form of a turtle formed the pivot for the churning rod to rest. Many articles came out of the ocean as the churning proceeded. One of the earlier objects to emerge was the poison *Kalakuta* (Halahala) which Shiva drank to save the ocean and the creatures inhabiting it, from total destruction. The ocean represents the universe and the poison represents death and destruction. Watching Shiva drink the poison, Parvati was worried and she held his throat so that the poison stuck to his throat and he got the epithet *Neelakantha*, the blue throated one, because the poison turns the victim blue. Throat is the symbol of *Akasha*, infinite space, the source of sound and speech; the poison stays there and does not come down to affect the mortal body.

After the poison had been got rid of by Shiva, Dhanvantari, the celestial physician, arose out of the milky ocean, carrying a bowl of the divine nectar, and a quarrel arose between the *daityas* and the *devatas* for its possession. To favour the *devatas*, Vishnu took the form of an enticingly beautiful woman called Mohini and, tȧking the bowl of nectar in her hands, started distributing the drink of immortality. After serving the drink to the *devatas*, she flew to the heavens, thus depriving the *daityas* of their share.

Vishnu in his form of Mohini, the Enchantress, was captivatingly beautiful and fame of her beauty spread far and wide. Shiva also heard of Mohini and wished to see her. Accompanied by Parvati, he visited her and, seeing her captivating curves, had lustful thoughts. He embraced Mohini and thus was created the Hari-Hara form of the God, i.e., half-Vishnu and half-Shiva. As Shiva embraced Mohini, Vishnu guessed his intentions and promply changed back into his normal form of a male. But by that time Shiva had already begotten a child from Mohini and this child was named Shasta. He grew up and became a great saint, He is also called Ayyappen.

Both nectar and poison are present in each individual soul. Only when the human soul can get rid of the poison, it can enjoy the nectar. Mind is like a deep ocean affected by both the good and the evil, the nectar and the poison. Varuna is the Lord of the ocean, master of the *asuras*, darkness, wind and cold, and Rudra-Shiva is the Lord of Fire which symbolises day, light, heat and truth. The world as well as the individual being is constituted of both these principles. He who can conquer darkness, bitterness and evil within him and can maintain his auspicious nature, is Shiva.

SHIVA BECOMES A WANDERER

Earlier Brahma had five heads. Four of his five heads face the four directions which symbolically are the source of the 4 *Vedas*. The eastern face symbolizes the *Rig Veda*, the western face, *Yajurveda*, the northe*n face, *Samaveda* and the southern face, the *Atharvaveda*. The fifth head was turned upwards. It represents not only scriptures but also arrogance. In his arrogance, Brahma moved about in the heavens, as if he was the source of all that mattered. His ego was so high that it created a dazzling lustre all around him, shadowing everything else.

According to a legend, Brahma propitiated Shiva for a long time by practising the severest of austerities. Pleased with his devotion, Shiva granted him a boon. Brahma asked Shiva to be born as his son. Shiva having already committed, had no choice but to agree to Brahma's demands. But not pleased with it, cursed Brahma to lose his fifth head for his audacity to approach him with such a proposal.

According to another version, Shiva cut off Brahma's fifth head as the latter committed incest with his own daughter. In either case, there was a fight between Brahma and Shiva. Shiva caught hold of his fifth head by its hair and cut it off. The hand that held the head of Brahma got paralysed and Shiva could not drop it. As time passed Shiva's hand got heavy with the weight of Brahma's head and Shiva started feeling weak. Seeing him thus weakened, Brahma took his revenge and sent a demon who rushed at Shiva. Shiva was unable to resist the onslaught of the demon and he fled to the city of Varanasi where he was absolved of the sin of killing a Brahmana as Brahma is the father of Brahmans and Shiva had cut off one of his heads. In Varanasi the fifth head of Brahma fell from the hands of Shiva and rejoined the body of Brahma.

Even though Brahma had regained his lost head, it was now his turn to curse Shiva and he cursed him to live as a wanderer and to beg for his living. Shiva is the only god of the holy trinity who has no celestial 'palace' to call his own. His abode is on Mount Kailash where he practises *yogic* austerities but otherwise roams around the universe as a homeless wanderer. He haunts the cremation grounds and dark and deserted places which are mostly frequented by ghosts, imps, witches, spirits and evil beings. On his wanderings, he carries a begging-bowl and a skull in his hands.

SHIVA MEETS ARJUNA

Like the other Hindu gods, Shiva also occasionally assumes human form. According to a story in the Mahabharata, Shiva disguised as a hunter once appeared to the Pandava prince Arjuna.

Arjuna had been exiled from his kingdom and was wandering in the forest. Realising that there was bound to be a serious conflict between the two families of the Kauravas and the Pandavas, Arjuna decided to propitiate Shiva and to obtain the boon of invincibility from him. With this in mind, he went to the Himalaya mountains and started practising austerities and penances, all the time keeping the image of Shiva constantly in his mind. His austerities became very severe and for many months he lived on nothing but air. This generated so much energy that there was a danger of the universe getting burnt to ashes. Seeing the danger, Shiva decided to grant Arjuna his boon and thus save the universe from total annihilation.

One day, soon after Shiva had decided to grant Arjuna his boon, while Arjuna was worshipping the Shiva-linga, a boar rushed at him. The martial-minded Arjuna forgot his worship and taking his bow and arrow, shot at the boar. About the same time another arrow shot by an unknown person also hit the boar. This was followed by the appearance of a hunter on the scene who started quarrelling with Arjuna for having spoiled his sport. Arjuna, on the other hand, felt that he was the aggrieved party and at that the two started fighting. In the midst of the fight, Arjuna remembered that he had forgotten to complete his worship of the *Lingam*. He took the garland of flowers intended for worship and threw it on the Shiva-linga. The garland missed its goal and instead of falling on the *linga*, it fell on the neck of the hunter. The hunter was actually Shiva in disguise. He now appeared before Arjuna in his true form and granted him his desired wish.

7

SHIVA AS ARDHANARISHVARA

There was a sage called Bhringi who was a great devotee of Shiva. But somehow he refused to accept Parvati as a goddess and would not offer her oblations. This infuriated Parvati as she being Shiva's female energy was really a part of him and naturally, therefore, expected to be also honoured along with him. But her protests at *rishi* Bhringi's indifference towards her evoked no response from him. To teach him a lesson, she removed her *shakti* or power from the *rishi* and the sage deprived of her support, became thin and emaciated. Becoming skin and bone, he could not even stand. Shiva, who is always benign towards his devotees, felt sorry for him and gave him a third leg as a prop so that the *rishi* could balance on his three skinny legs.

When Parvati found this out, she was infuriated both at Shiva and at Bhringi. Bhringi still circumbulated only Shiva. To force him to circumbulate her also, Parvati joined herself permanently to Shiva's body and thus Shiva became Ardhanarishvara, half-man and half-woman. By doing so, she thought that when the *rishi* next circumbulated her husband Shiva, he would have no choice but to circumbulate her also, as now they were of one body. But Bhringi proved more crafty than she had realised. He took the form of a wasp and came out of their joined navels and thus cheated Parvati by only circumbulating Shiva.

According to another version regarding the creation of half-man half-woman form of Shiva, Shiva Ardhanarishvara was created as Parvati was jealous of Lakshmi because her husband Vishnu, always carried the mark *Shrivasta,* the

symbol of Lakshmi, on his chest. Parvati one day complained
about this to Shiva and said that he neglected her. To
appease Parvati, Shiva gave half of his body to her and thus
became *Ardhanarishvara*.

The two universal parents, the father and the Mother,
Heaven and earth, are symbolised in the half-male and half
female aspect of Shiva. The male half is Agni and the female
half is Soma. Heaven is father and Earth is mother,
Dyava_Prithivi. Heaven symbolises the immortal world of
the *Devatas* and the earth, the mortal world of matter. These
are the two eternal symbols of life and matter,the duality
of life and death, without either of which creation cannot
go on.

RAVANA SHAKES MOUNT KAILASH

Once Ravana, the demon King of Lanka, visited
Sharavana, the birth place of Karttikeya,on the Himalayas.
Shiva was sporting with Parvati on the mountain, and a
dwarf with the face of a monkey stopped Ravana saying that
Shiva was with Parvati and not even a god was permitted
to go there. Enraged at the audacity of a monkey faced dwarf,
Ravana hit him. At this, the dwarf, who was really Shiva
in disguise, cursed him and said that he would be defeated
by monkey-faced beings, and was killed by Ramachandra and
his monkey hosts, the *Vanar_Sena*.

To get back to the story, Ravana, after hitting the dwarf,
started shaking Mr.Kailash on which Shiva was sitting with
Parvati. With the shaking of the mountain, rocks, boulders
and even mountain tops started falling, trees got uprooted
making a deafening noise. The earth quaked and rivers
flowed over their banks. Parvati got frightened at the
upheavel and clung to Shiva for protection. Shiva asked her
not to feel frightened but since Parvati continued to shake
with fear, to reassure her, he pressed the mountain with
his big toe. The mountain instantly stopped shaking and at
the same time Ravana got trapped under it.

Many years passed thus with Ravana trapped under the
abode of Shiva and did not know how to extricate himself.
His friends and admirers advised him to propitiate Shiva

and to ask for forgiveness. Ravana subdued his anger and propitiated Shiva for one thousand years till pleased with his devotion, Shiva extricated him from under the mountain. Ravana from that time onwards became a great devotee of Shiva.

The form of Shiva taking compassion on Ravana in spite of his insolence at shaking Mt. Kailash, is called *Ravananugrahamurti*.

Kailash mountain represents the higher centres of the mind where Shiva and Parvati remain in eternal union. Mt. Kailash is the place where the *Kundalini* yoga, i.e., the Great Serpent Power which embraces the body of Shiva and converts its poison into ambrosial drops is present. Parvati represents the energy of the body called *Kundalini*. Ravana in his foolish pride thought that he could disturb the eternal union of mind and soul represented by Shiva and Parvati. Shiva, by virtue of his conquering the God of love, is above all temptation and, therefore, the only salvation left for Ravana was the mercy shown to him by Shiva because only one led by temptation can be destroyed, not one who is above it.

THE DESCENT OF GANGA

Once a group of demons were harassing the hermits by disturbing their sacred ascetic duties. In the day time, they would be chased into the ocean. But in the darkness of the night, they would emerge from the ocean and start harassing the holy sages again. The hermits, in desperation appealed to *rishi* Agastya. Agastya known for his gastronomic powers, drank all the waters of the ocean. Though this was done in all good faith, it resulted in depriving the world of the necessary water needed for sustenance and the earth became parched and dry.

This terrible drought was brought to an end by the ascetic merit of another holy man called Bhagiratha. Bhagiratha was a pious king who was a direct descendant of Manu Vaivasvata of the solar dynasty. Sixty thousand of his ancestors had been burnt to ashes by sage Kapila for having disturbed his meditation. Bhagiratha wished to perform the

shraddha ceremony for his dead ancestors, so that their souls
would rest in peace and for this ceremony, he required holy
water. Since there was no water on the earth now, he went
to Shiva's sacred city called *Gokarna* and with unflinching
devotion, practised austerities there. Brahma was attracted
by his ascetic fervour and manifesting himself, he granted
Bhagiratha a boon. Bhagiratha asked for the celestial Ganga
to descend to the earth so that its life-giving waters would
flow through the land. Brahma agreed to grant the boon
but said that without the grace of Shiva, it was not possible.
If the torrential waters of the Ganga came cascading straight
down to the earth, their gigantic weight and force would
cleave the earth and shatter it to bits. But if Shiva would
receive the full weight of the river on his head, this
catastrophe would be averted. He further suggested to
Bhagiratha to continue his austerities to please Shiva. .

Bhagiratha understood the nature of the stupendous task
facing him. Shiva the arch-ascetic, sitting in solitary
splendour on a remote summit of the Himalayas, steeped
in pure and perfect meditation, absorbed in the Supreme void
of his own divine essence, was almost unapproachable. To
draw his attention and to appease him was no easy matter.
But even so, Bhagiratha undertook this stupendous task and
went to the Himalayas and continued his ascetic austerities
and penances with his mind and will concentrated solely on
Shiva, till Shiva eventually appeared before the saint and
agreed to receive the celestial river Ganga on his head.

Shiva received the cascading current of the Ganga on
his matted hair piled high on his head. The hair ensnared
and delayed the progress of the river which, in meandering
through the labyrinth of his hair, lost its force and then
gently descended to the Himalayas in seven streams from
where it flowed to the plains bestowing its life-giving waters
to the parched earth. And that is why the anthropomorphic
image of Ganga is shown in the matted hair of Shiva. Shiva
is called *Gangadhara*, the bearer of Ganga. Being born of
the Himalayas, Ganga is considered the elder sister of Shiva's
consort Uma.

Shiva's semen was thrown into the river Ganga and she
unable to bear it, cast it on her banks. After being thrown

away from the womb of Ganga, the semen took the form
of a child of Shiva who was called Skanda. Therefore, Ganga
is also considered as a wife of Shiva for having retained
for a while his seed in her womb.

SHIVA IS KALANTAKA

Shiva is Kalantaka, conqueror of death, Kala or Time.
Markandeya, a young boy, a devotee of Shiva was destined
to die at the age of 16. Since he did not want to die so
young, he clasped the *Linga* he was worshipping when the
messenger of Yama, the Lord of death approached him. Shiva
pleased with Markandeya's devotion, arrived at that time
and defeated *Kala* (death), and bestowed eternal youth on
Markandeya. Since then Shiva is called *Kalantaka,* conqueror
of *Kala,* Time.

8

SHAKTI, THE AUSPICIOUS GODDESS

For full one hundred years, there was a war between the celestials and the demons, i.e., the elements of goodness and evil. At that time, Mahisha was the Lord of the *asuras* (demons) and Indra of the *devatas* (celestials). The *asuras* being more powerful, the army of the *devatas* was vanquished by them in no time and Mahisha became Indra. The defeated *devatas*, with Brahma as their leader, went to Shiva and Vishnu and told them of the atrocities perpetuated by Mahisha. Mahisha held jurisdiction over the Sun, Indra, Agni, Vayu, Soma, Yama and Varuna and over all lesser deities. Thrown out of heaven by the evil-souled Mahisha, the *devatas* wandered on earth like mortals and prayed to the Supreme gods Shiva and Vishnu to devise some means by which Mahishasura could be destroyed.

Hearing of the atrocities committed by Mahisha on the *devatas*, both Shiva and Vishnu were incensed. Then from the mouths of Brahma, Vishnu, Shiva and from the body of Indra and lesser *devatas*, issued great energy and all these energies amalgamated. This unparalleled intense energy, born of the bodies of all *devatas* and burning like a mountain, pervaded the three worlds with its light and gathering into one, became a woman. From Shiva's energy was developed her face; from Yama's energy, her hair; her arms were made from Vishnu's energy and the Moon's energy formed her breasts; her waist came from Indra's energy; Varuna's energy gave her legs Earth's energy formed her hips; Brahma's

energy gave her toes; from Vasus' energy were formed her
hands; Kubera's energy formed her nose; her teeth grew by
Prajapati's energy and she got her three eyes by Agni's
energy. Her eyebrows were the energy of the two twilights
(dusk and dawn) and her ears were made from Vayu's energy.
This woman formed from the collective energies of all the
devatas became the auspicious Goddess and was named
Shakti.

Gazing at this female form which had sprung from the
energies of the various *devatas,* the immortals felt great joy.
Shiva drew a trident from his own trident and gave it to
her; Vishnu gave her a Discus pulling it out of his own
Discus; Agni a spear; Maruta gave her a bow and a quiver
full of arrows and the thousand-eyed Indra gave her a
thunder-bolt pulled out of his own thunderbolt and a bell
from his elephant Airavata. Yama gave her a rod from his
own rod of fate, and the Lord of waters Varuna, gave her
a noose and a conch; Prajapati gave her a necklace of beads
and Brahma an earthen water-pot; the Sun bestowed his own
rays on all the pores of her skin and Kala (destiny) gave
her a sword and a spotless shield; the Ocean of Milk, a
spotless necklace of pearls and a pair of undecaying
garments. Vishvakarman gave her a celestial crest-jewel, a
pair of ear-rings, bracelets, a brilliant half-moon ornament,
armlets, a pair of shining anklets, necklaces of the finest
make, gems and rings for all her fingers, also a brightly
polished axe, weapons of many types and armour that could
not be pierced.

The ocean gave her a garland of unfading flowers as well
as lotus flowers. From Himavat she got a lion as a vehicle
and precious, shining gems. Kubera gave her a cup of wine
and Shesha, the Lord of serpents, gave her a serpent necklace
which was adorned with large gems.

Thus honoured by all the *devatas* and resplendent with
the gifts of ornaments and weapons, the goddess uttered a
terrifying loud roar blended with horse laugh which shook
the whole universe. The penetrating roar echoed, the world
shook, the seas trembled, the earth quaked and the
mountains moved. Confident in her strength and power, the
gods exclaimed: "Conquer thou!"

Seeing such great agitation in the three worlds, Mahishasura gathered all his armies and his weapons and rushed towards the great uprising.

From a distance he saw the goddess pervading the universe with her light and the earth bowing before her. The Goddess shook *Patala* with a mere twang of her bow string and her thousand arms reached the very end of the sky. A battle began between the Goddess and the *asuras*. Some of the important generals of Mahishasura who fought the Goddess were Chiksura, Chamara, Udagra, Maha-bana, Asi-loman, Ugra-darshana and Vidata. The battle fought was fierce and every region of the sky was illuminated with the weapons hurled by each party. Goddess Chandika cut the weapons hurled at her into pieces almost as if it was a game she was playing.

The lion which the Goddess was riding, however, was enraged and stalked through the armies of the *asuras* like fire coursing through a forest. From the breath of the Goddess, troops by the thousand were born. These newly formed troops raised a din on the battlefield by beating drums and blowing conches. They fought with weapons like axes, javelins, swords, and halberds and destroyed the *asura* bands. At the same time Goddess Chandika, also called Ambika, slaughtered the *asuras* by the hundred with her weapons, the trident, club, spear and the sword. Some *asuras* were bewitched by the ringing of her bell, others were dragged on the earth by her noose, some were killed by her spear and mace or cut into pieces by her trident and arrows. Rivers of blood flowed from the *asuras* killed by her. Just as a pile of grass and timber is consumed by fire in no time, similarly the Goddess in no time annihilated the army of the *asuras*.

The powerful *asura* general Chiksura advanced towards the Goddess. In great wrath he sent a shower of arrows at Ambika almost as clouds deluge the summit of Mt.Meru with a shower of rain. The Goddess cut asunder the arrows shot at her. She killed his horses and charioteers, split his bow and banner and with swift missiles, pierced his limbs.

When all his army and weapons were made useless, *asura* Chiksura came with the swiftness of wind and hit the lion of the Goddess on his head with his sharp-edged sword, and

struck the Goddess on her arm. But his sword was shattered
to pieces as it touched her arms. At this the eyes of the
asura blazed with anger and picking up his spear, he flung
it at the Goddess who was also called *Bhadrakali*.
Bhadrakali, who was shining like the orb of the sun, hurled
her spear at the spear of the *asura* that was coming towards
her like a missile and shattered it into a hundred fragments
in mid air.

Seeing the army of the *asuras* getting annihilated by the
Goddess, *asura* Mahisha took his original form of a buffalo
and lifted the mountains high. The earth was crushed to
pieces and the oceans, lashed by his tail, overflowed in every
direction. The clouds pierced by his swaying horns were
scattered and the mountains fell from the sky.

Chandika, swollen with rage, looked at the *asura* as he
rushed at her and she flung her noose over him and bound
him fast. The *asura* changed his buffalo shape and became
a lion. When the Goddess was going to cut off his head,
he took the form of a man carrying a scimitar in his hands.
But the Goddess pierced this man along with his scimitar
and shield. The *asura* next became a huge elephant and
tugged at her lion with his trunk and hooted loudly. At this
the Goddess cut off his trunk. The *asura* again assumed his
buffalo form and shook the three worlds. The Goddess was
greatly enraged at his behaviour and drinking a sublime
beverage laughed at him with her shining red eyes. The
asura meanwhile kept on hurling mountains at her and
attacking her with all his strength and valour. The Goddess
spoke to him and said:

"Roar, roar, you fool. Your end has come. While I drink
this celestial beverage, you can continue to hurl weapons
at me. I will slay you and then it will be the turn of the
devatas to roar with joy."

Saying this, the Goddess leapt forward and sat on the
back of the *Asura* Mahisha. She kicked him on the neck
with her feet and struck him hard with her spear. Assailed
thus by the Goddess, he half issued from his own mouth
but before he could emerge and escape again, the Goddess
struck off his head.

At the death of their king, the *daitya* army perished amidst great lamentations. The army of the celestials shouted with unrestrained joy and the *devatas* and *rishis* praised the Goddess; the *gandharvas* burst into songs and the *apsaras* started dancing. Eulogised by the *devatas, rishis* and mortals, the Goddess gave them a boon and said that whenever they would sing her praise and eulogise her, she would come to their rescue. Saying this, she vanished.

Mahishasura had been killed and his army routed. The killing of Mahishasura gave the Goddess the epithet *Mahishasuramardini.*

SHUMBHA AND NISHUMBA

After Mahishasura was killed, peace reigned in the three worlds for some time. But it was not to last long and once again the universe was in turmoil. This time the reasons for the upheaval were the brothers Shumbha and Nishumbha who, with their strength and pride robbed Indra of the sovereignty of the three worlds. They usurped the dignity of the Sun and the dominion of the Moon, Kubera, Yama and Varuna. They took away the authority that Vayu possessed and pervaded Agni's sphere of action. The *devatas,* deprived of their dominion, decided to seek the help of the Goddess to regain their kingdom. Making this resolve, they went to Himavat, the Lord of the mountains, and hymned his praise and praise of the Goddess, who in actual fact is the collective energy of all the *devatas.*

While the *devatas* were thus engaged in offereing praise to Goddess, Parvati, the consort of Shiva, came to bathe in the waters of the Ganga. Hearing the hymns of praise, she approached the *devatas* and asked whom they were propitiating. Before the *devatas* could even answer, the auspicious Goddess sprang out of Parvati's body and said:

"I know that you are propitiating me because you have been defeated by the *daityas* Shumbha and Nishumbha."

Because the auspicious Goddess in this form issued from the body of Parvati, she is also known as *Kaushiki.*

Chanda and Munda, the servants of the *daityas* Shumbha and Nishumbha, saw Ambika, the auspicious Goddess,

displaying her sublime and captivating forms before the
devatas and they went and praised her beauty to Shumbha.

"She is a gem among women," they said, "and has a
beautiful body which shines with a lustre unsurpassed by
any other." Chanda and Munda, after praising the Goddess,
incited Shumbha and Nishumbha to seize her.

Even though Shumbha had not seen Ambika, he decided
to marry her only on the strength of the praise that he heard
from his servants. With this in mind, he sent his general
Sugriva to her as a messenger after instructing him thus:
"Go and tell her my wishes and desires but conduct the
matter softly and in a manner that she herself comes to
me, without my having to use force."

Asura general Sugriva on instructions from his master
went to the Godddess and started praising him to her. He
told her how strong Shumbha was and that he was the Lord
of the three worlds and then made his offer of marriage on
his master's behalf. The Goddess replied:

"I agree with you that your master is very powerful and
has become the Lord of the three worlds. It is also true he
possesses the choicest gems of the entire universe but I am
sorry to disappoint him. I have taken a vow that I shall
only marry a man who defeats me in single combat, who
is my match in strength and who can force my pride from
me."

The messenger answered: "O Goddess, be not proud of
your strength and beauty. No one has so far been able to
stand up and face the brothers Shumbha and Nishumbha
in battle. When even gods like Indra could not succeed
against them, then how can you a mere woman fight him
single handed? I only hope for your sake that ultimately
you won't have to be dragged before him for that sure would
shatter your dignity."

The messenger of Shumbha was filled with indignation
at the pride of the Goddess but had no choice but to go
and convey to Shumbha the attitude of the Goddess.

The *asura* monarch Shumbha had not expected such a
haughty reply from the Goddess. Sure of his strength because
of his earlier conquests, he was confident that the Goddess
would willingly agree to be his wife. In fact, he thought that

she would consider it an honour. He was incensed to hear the reply that Ambika had given to his proposal of marriage and ordered his commander Dhumra-locana to march against the Goddess with his army and to bring her to him, if necessary by force. He instructed his general that if Ambika was dragged by her hair, she was sure to be unnerved and then it would be easy to bring her. He also ordered him to kill anyone who stood in his way and that no clemency was to be shown to her attendants.

To seize the Goddess was not that simple a matter as Shumbha had thought it to be, and his general Dhumra-lochana, not taking any chances, decided to take with him an army of sixty thousand *asuras*. On approaching the Himalayas, he saw the Goddess stationed on the snowy peaks and addressed her thus:

"Come to the *asuras* Shumbha and Nishumbha willingly. But if you will not approach my lord with affection of your own free will, then I will have to take you to them by force, if necessary, by pulling you by your hair."

The Goddess replied calmly that since he had come with an army to seize her, she had no choice but to be seized by force and urged him to fight with her.

Dhumra-lochana had thought that it would be no problem to capture her. After all, she was only a woman. So thus challenged by her, he rushed towards her with intentions of seizing her by force. But Ambika had just to shout at him and he was reduced to ashes. Seeing their leader thus destroyed, the army of the *asura* poured a volley of sharp arrows at her and also hurled spears, javelins and axes to kill her. This enraged the lion of Ambika who was carrying her on his back. Shaking his mane in anger and uttering a deafening roar, he fell on the *asuras* and slaughtered them by tearing out their entrails with his claws and drank up their blood. He destroyed the army of the *daityas* in no time.

When Shumbha, the Lord of the *daityas,* heard that his army led by Dhumra-lochana was destroyed, he ordered his servants Chanda and Munda to take an army to bring Ambika to him, and if it became necessary, to bind her hand and foot and drag her to him, and if that was not posssible, then to kill her.

Chanda and Munda marched towards the Goddess with a large army of the *daityas*. They saw her seated on a lion on the golden peak of the Himalayas. On seeing her, some of the *daityas* made an effort to seize her and others approached her with bent bows and drawn swords.

Seeing them approach the golden peak of the Himalayas, the Goddess uttered a loud cry which was in fact her wrath against them and her face became dark as ink. From her forehead full of frowns, issued a Goddess of terrible countenance. She was Kali, the terrible. Kali was armed with a sword and a noose and was holding a many-coloured skull-topped staff called *Khatvanga*. She was decorated with a garland of skulls and her skin was thin, dry and wrinkled. She was dressed in only a tiger skin which gave her a frightening appearance. Her mouth was exceedingly wide with a lolling tongue. Her eyes were red and deeply sunken in their pits and her roar filled the far regions of the sky. Kali fell upon the army of the *asuras*, slaughtering and devouring them and grounding to pulp their chariots and weapons. Chanda and Munda rushed towards her when they saw her killing and maiming their army, but the Goddess cut off their heads. For killing Chanda and Munda, she came to be called *Chamunda*.

After the *daityas* Chanda and Munda were slain, Shumbha ordered various categories of *daityas* and *danavas* to fight the Goddess. These included eighty-six *daityas* eighty-four Kambus and their armies, fifty *asura* families, hundred families of Dhaumras, Kalakas, Daurhritas, Mauryas, etc.

Issuing these commands, Shumbha, attended by thousands of soldiers, went to attack Chandika. Seeing this formidable army, Chandika made a deafening noise by the twang of her bowstring and by ringing her bell. Her lion also roared loudly and hearing this noise which filled the four quarters of the universe, the enraged *daitya* army surrounded the Goddess who was seated on her lion. At this, the different energies of the gods like Brahma, Vishnu, Shiva, Kumara and Indra, issued from their bodies and taking their own distinctive forms, carrying their weapons and riding their own vehicles to fight the *asuras,* went to the aid of

Chandika. They were determined to destroy the enemies of
the gods forever. Leading this group of goddesses was
Brahmani, the energy of Brahma. She was riding a vehicle
drawn by swans and carrying a rosary and an earthen pot.
Shiva's energy called Maheshvari arrived next, seated on a
bull and holding a trident and wearing a girdle of snakes
and adorned with a moon. There was Kaumari, also called
Ambika, the energy of Kumara. She was riding a peacock
and carried a spear in her hand. Taking the form of Kaumari,
she advanced to fight the *daityas*. Likewise, Vishnu's energy
called Vaishnavi came seated on Garuda. She was holding
a conch, a discus, club, bow and scimitar. The energy of
Vishnu in his Boar incarnation, i.e., the Varaha form called
varahi, also came. Narasimha's energy assuming a body like
that of Narasimha arrived adorned with a cluster of
constellations which he had hurled down by tossing his mane.
Similarly, Indrani, the energy of Indra, arrived seated on
an elephant and possessing a thousand eyes and carrying
the thunderbolt in her hands. All these energies called Sapta-
matrikas surrounded Shivaa, the female energy of Shiva
Maheshvara and addressed Chandika:
"Let the *asuras* be slain forthwith. This is my wish."
Hearing this, the energy of Chandika, terrifying and
fierce to look at and howling like a hundred jackals, issued
from the body of Chandika and requested Shivaa, the female
energy of Shiva, to be her messenger. Shivaa was asked to
go to the *daityas* Shumbha and Nishumbha and their
followers who had assembled to attack the Great Goddess
to warn them that, if they wished to live, they could go
to *Patala* and abide there, and let Indra rule over the three
worlds again. But if they were proud and haughty and wished
to fight, then they would be annihilated and the jackals of
the Goddess would feed on their flesh. Because the Goddess
had appointed Shivaa as her ambassador, she came to be
called *Shivaduti*.
Hearing this message of Chandika, the *asuras* went
where the Goddess known by the name of *Katyayani* stood
and rained a volley of arrows, javelins and spears on her.
But the Goddess similingly cut these weapons into pieces.
As the great Goddess went into the battlefield, she was

preceeded by Kali who kept on tearing the *asuras* to pieces
and crushing them with her staff that had a skull on its
top. Brahmani by sprinkling holy water from her earthen
water pot, the Kamandalu, made the *asuras* lose courage
and thus made them weak. Maheshvari slew the *daityas* with
her trident, and Vashnavi with her Discus; Kaumari, the
female energy of Kumara, slew them with her javelin; Indra's
energy, Indrani, tore the *daityas* to pieces by her thunderbolt.
Varahi, the energy of Varaha avatara of Vishnu, shattered
the *daityas* to bits with blows from her snout and wounded
them in the breasts with tusks, or tore them to pieces by
her Discus. The energy of Narasimha roamed about in the
battlefield, devouring other *asuras,* tearing them by her
claws and filled the universe with her deafening roar. Thus
the *daityas* and the *danavas* were killed in hundreds and
blood flowed from them forming streams. The *asuras*
demoralised at the violent laughs of Shivadhuti, fell down
on the earth and were devoured by her. The *asuras* perished
one by one due to the diffferent means adopted for their
destruction by the enraged Mothers.

When the *asura* chief Rakta-bija saw the surviving
asuras afraid of the Mothers, fleeing from the battlefield,
his blood boiled with anger and he came into the battle
ground to fight. He was given the name Rakta-bija because
an *asura* was born from every drop of his blood that fell
on the ground. Rakta-bija first attacked Indrani, the female
energy of Indra and hit her hard with a club. Indra's shakti
retaliated and struck him with her thunderbolt but soon as
many *asuras* arose from as many drops of blood that flowed
from his body. These new-born *asuras* were all like him in
appearance, courage, strength and valour. It was not only
Indrani who attacked Rakta-bija. Like her, Vishnu's *shakti*
struck him with her Discus; Kumara's energy struck the
asura with her spear; Varaha's with her sword and
Maheshvari's with her trident. But instead of killing him,
asuras by the thousand arose from his blood that fell on
the ground and they also joined the rest of the army in
attacking the mothers and goddesses. Seeing such a
formidable army of *asuras* out of Rakta-bija's wounds, the
devatas got terrified.

When the gods were dejected and demoralised, Chandika spoke to Kali and said: "O Chamunda, stretch wide your mouth and swallow the *asuras* who are really the blood that has come out of Rakta-bija's wounds inflicted by me. Go and roam around the battlefield and devour the *asuras* who have sprung from the blood of Rakta-bija. When his blood would thus ebb away, Rakta-bija would meet his death. While these fierce-looking beings will be devoured by you, at the same time, no others would be produced."

Saying this, the Goddess hit Rakta-bija with great fury and the blood that came out was swallowed by Kali. Rakta-bija also struck Chandika with his club but it caused her no pain and Kali or Chandika continued to drink the blood of the *asura* from wherever it flowed due to the multiple injuries inflicted on him by the Goddess. Soon the *asura* became bloodless and died. At his death, the *devatas* were full of joy and the mother goddesses started dancing.

After the death of Rakta-bija and other demons, Shumbha and Nishumbha gave way to unbounded wrath. They were full of indignation at the slaughter of their armies and rushed to kill the Goddess. A desperate combat took place between the Goddess and the two *asura* brothers. The *asuras* sent a shower of arrows towards her but Chandika sent her missiles to split the arrows in mid-air, even before they reached her. Nishumbha then picked up a scimitar and a shield with a horse-shoe shaped arrow. Next the *asura* sent his missile towards her but she split it with her Discus. The *Danava* Nishumbha puffed with rage and seized a dart to strike her, but even before he could hit her, she shattered it with a blow of her fist. Then he aimed his club against Chandika, but the Goddess reduced it to ashes with her trident. Lastly, the *Daitya* advanced towards her with his battle-axe but the Goddess attacked him with arrows and he was finally killed.

After Nishumbha had been slain and his army slaughtered, Shumbha spoke angrily to the Goddess and said: "O Durga, you are full of arrogance and pride. You are fighting with great haughtiness because you depend on the strength of other goddesses."

Goddess Durga replied: "You vile one! Which other goddess is there besides me? These mother goddesses that you see are a part of me and derive their power from me. See, they are even now entering into me."

Durga had barely finished speaking when all the goddesses became absorbed into her and Durga alone remained. Then Durga spoke again:

"I existed before with my divine power in many forms but that divine power is now drawn back into myself and now I stand alone. You can see for yourself that all the goddesses were only an image of me, my different manifestations."

Durga had not even finished clarifying who the goddesses were when a fierce battle started all over again between her and Shumbha, while all the *devatas* and *asuras* looked on. A shower of arrows rained from both the Goddess and the *Asura* and sharp weapons and missiles clashed in combat, at which all the three worlds trembled in fear. But the Supreme Goddess broke these heavy weapons almost as if in play. This battle between the energies of good and evil lasted with unabated fury for a very long time. Chandika pushed the *daitya* with such force that he fell on the ground. But he rose quickly and sprang forward, seized the Goddess and flew into the sky. Even without a support, Chandika fought with him and, after a prolonged close combat, threw him on to the earth. Before he could get up, Chandika pierced him with a dart and killed him. When the lifeless body of Shumbha fell on the earth, tremors were felt in all corners of the earth and even the seas and mountains shook.

With the death of the evil *daitya*, the universe became peaceful, the sky became pure and clear and peace reigned on earth once again. The rivers no longer overflowed their banks and the clouds, which earlier were full of fire, became gentle and cool breezes blew. The *devatas* were full of joy, the *gandharvas* sang and the *apsaras* danced gaily. The sun grew brilliant, the sacred fires blazed freely and favourable breezes blew all around.

When all the dreaded demons had been killed, the *devatas* and *rishis* sang Durga's praise and eulogised her. Pleased with their prayers, the Goddess spoke to them thus:

"I am pleased with your devotion. Choose whatever boon you desire and I shall grant it."

The gods asked for the destruction of the demons who were their enemies, and for the removal of ills of the three worlds.

The Goddess answered: "When the 28th *yuga* arrives in the Vaivasta Manvantara, two other powerful *asuras* will be born, as strong as Shumbha and Nishumbha. I shall then be born as Yashoda's daughter in the house of a cowherd called Nanda. While dwelling in the Vindhya mountains, I shall slay these two *asuras*. Once again I shall become incarnate on this earth to kill the Vaiprachitta *danavas*. After slaying these *danavas,* my teeth shall become red like the pomegranate. Because of my blood-red teeth, I shall be praised on earth and in heaven as *Rakta-dantika,* the red-toothed one.

"There would be a lapse of a hundred years before I shall again come back to earth, but this time I shall not be born of a womb. During these hundred years, rain will fail on the earth and there will be a severe drought. *Rishis* will praise me and I shall behold them with my hundred eyes for which mankind will eulogise me as *Shatakshi,* the hundred-eyed one.

"Next, O gods, I shall support the whole world with life-sustaining vegetables and herbs, and plants will grow during the rains out of my own body. At that time I shall become famous on the earth by the name *Shakambhari,* i.e., the herb-nourisher and during that period, I shall slay the *asura* Durgama.

"Once again to save the pious and the good, I shall assume a terrifying-looking form on Mt. Himavat and shall destroy the *rakshasas* who inflict atrocities on pious people. Because of my strength and terrible demeanour, I shall be reverently lauded as *Bhimadevi.*

"When the *asura* Arunaksha will create trouble in the three worlds, I shall take the form of a bee and for the good of the world, I shall slay the *asura*. I shall then be praised as *Bhramari,* the bee-like goddess.

"Thus, whenever trouble shall arise due to the *daityas* and the *danavas,* I shall reincarnate in some form or other and shall destroy evil."

Then the gods and the *rishis* eulogised the Goddess thus:

"The adorable everlasting Goddess safeguards the world. The universe is bewitched by her. She is the Creator of the universe. When sought after, she bestows knowledge and when gratified by the devotees, bestows property. The egg of Brahma is pervaded by her. She is Mahakali at Mahakala and destroys all evil. She is Mahamari at the fated time; she is Creation, the unborn; She the Eternal one giving stability to created beings. She is Lakshmi bestowing prosperity on men while She abides with them and becomes Alakshmi, the goddess of ill-fortune, when she is absent from people's homes and in that form she destroys them. When praised and worshipped with flowers and incense, perfumes and other offerings, she bestows wealth, sons and a right-thinking, clear mind. She is Vishnu's illusive power. When propitiated by men, she bestows enjoyment, heaven and final release from the cycle of birth and rebirth."

GAJASURA IS SLAIN

Gajasura created by Brahma was a follower of Vishnu. Brahma once wished to perform a sacrifice on his body and Gajasura, being a true devotee of him, readily agreed. When Brahma was going to perform the sacrifice, he found Gajasura very unstable. To stabilise him, Brahma ordered Dharma to place a stone on the head of Gajasura and to stand on that stone. But Gajasura continued to be unstable. Then Vishnu himself offered to stand on the stone placed on the head of Gajasura. As he did that, the stone became motionless. He then gave the *asura* a murti of himself for worship.

Gajasura was the son of Mahishasura and he was incensed at Durga for killing his father and decided to take revenge. First, he decided to become strong enough so that he could fight Shiva and his consort Durga. With this in mind, he started practising severe austerities in order to propitiate Brahma. For the performance of his austerities, he went to the Himalayas. His austerities consisted of keeping his arms uplifted for an endless period, his eyes fixed on the sky and standing only on his big toes. This penance went on for thousands of years.

As a result of his severe penance, the body of the *asura* shone bright like the sun at the time of the final dissolution. The fire of his penance originated from his head and the smoke spread all around the three worlds. Because of the severe austerities that he was performing, the rivers overflowed their banks and the waters of the seas heaved and churned as if a major catastrophe had occurred. The stars fell from the sky and the four quarters blazed. Seeing these omens, the *devatas* got frightened. Afraid of Gajasura's austerities, they approached Brahma for help. Brahma appeared before Gajasura and to help the *devatas* offered him a boon on condition that he would stop his austerities and thus save the universe from total annihilation.

Gajasura asked: "I agree to your condition. Let me be immune to destruction both from mortals and also from any other forms of creatures who are lustful. Let me be powerful, invincible to celestials, guardians of the world and from all other creatures. I should be killed only by one who is free of lust."

Brahma was surprised at the strangeness of the request. However, he granted Gajasura the boon he craved. After getting his cherished boon of invulnerability, Gajasura became very powerful. He conquered the three worlds and made the celestials subservient to him, and reigned supreme. He enjoyed earthly pleasures to the maximum but since he failed to conquer his senses, he was never satiated. He was arrogant and proud of his affluence. He slighted the sacred scriptures and became evil-minded after which he started harassing the *rishis* and other holy sages. Recollecting the death of his father Mahishasura, he tortured all righteous beings.

Gajasura's atrocities on men, *devatas* and semi-divine beings reached a peak. Once he decided to go to Shiva's city. When he arrived there, the *devatas* and sages, out of fright, took refuge in Shiva and complained to him:

"Gajasura has gone to your city and is inflicting pain on all. When he walks, the earth shakes by his weight, trees are uprooted by the velocity of the wind that rises as he walks and mountains are reduced to powder by his strong arms. The oceans get so agitated that waves arise as high as the mountains and the rivers overflow their banks. With his height of nine thousand *yojanas* he is like a mountain in terror. Please protect us from him."

Thus requested by the celestials, Shiva came forward with intentions to kill Gajasura. Gajasura was a strong and powerful demon. A fierce battle took place and various kinds of weapons were used by both of them against each other. Gajasura's roar deafened all living creatures for miles around but in spite of his strength, he stood no chance before the might of Shiva who always kills evil. Shiva raised his trident to pierce him and afraid of dying, Gajasura the elephant-bodied demon, sang the praises of Shiva. He said that to die at the hands of Shiva was equal to receiving glory. Pleased with his eulogy, Shiva offered him a boon.

Gajasura asked" "If you are indeed pleased with me, wear this hide of mine which has been sanctified by the fire of your trident. Even though the hide has been scorched by the fire issuing from your trident, it has not got burnt. If you are pleased with me, then let your name be *Krittivasas,* one clad in an elephant hide. And thus Shiva came to be called *Krittivaseshvara.*

Because of his *asuric* or demoniac nature, Gajasura started destroying the universal rhythm with his wild, uncontrolled and unharnessed energy. Shiva, the only one who was untouched by lust, killed him to regulate the creative activity. Shiva could do that because he was the destroyer of Kamadeva, the god of lust.

9

NATARAJA

Once Shiva descended on the earth and found people arguing among themselves about the existence of the Supreme Soul. Seeing Shiva, a stranger, and not realising who he was, they threw a snake at him which Shiva caught in his hands and wrapped it round his neck like a scarf and by doing so, he absorbed within himself, the snake like cunning of mankind. The snake symbolises the transmigration of souls from one body to another. The soul is eternal and it casts off the worn out body like a worn out garment and enters another body, just as the snake sloughs off his outer skin. This snake is a symbolic representation of Shiva as the Supreme Soul.

Having failed in their attempts at killing Shiva by throwing a poisonous snake at him, the assembled gathering sent a tiger to devour him. Shiva skinned the tiger with his finger nail and wrapped the skin round him and thus merged the tiger like fury of mankind within him. Lastly, the mortals sent a demon, *Apasmara Purush* to fight Shiva. This demon represents forgetfulness symbolising the ignorance of man. To conquer this demon is to attain true wisdom and release from the bondage of the world. Shiva crushed the demon under his foot and started dancing on the trampled body, and thus crushed the evil of mankind and maintained the balance of the world rhythm in his dance.

Shiva in the dance pose is known as *Nataraja,* the Lord
of dances. He created one hundred and eight dance forms.

Iconographically, *Nataraja* is shown with four arms. The
two normal ones are in the elephant pose *Gajahasta mudra*
and in the gesture of fearlessness, i.e.*abhayahasta mudra*
respectively. The other two arms hold the drum and the fire.
For the beating of the rhythm while dancing, Shiva's upper
right hand carries an hour-glass shaped drum. The sound
it produces is speech which conveys revelation, tradition,
magic and divine truth. Sound is also associated with Ether
which is the first of the five elements: ether, air, fire, water
and earth. Together sound and ether signify the first
creation, the productive energy of the Absolute.

The opposite hand is in the *ardhacandra mudra,* the half
moon posture of the fingers and it bears a tongue of flame
which element denotes destruction of the world. At the end
of the *Kali-yuga, Agni* (fire) will destroy creation and will
itself get quenched by the ocean of the Void. Thus by the
balance of the hands of the Cosmic Dancer, *Damuru* (sound)
against *Agni* (fire) are the two opposites, ceaseless creation
and destruction.

The second right hand is in the *abhaya mudra,* fear not,
which gesture bestows protection and peace, while the left
hand lifted across his chest, points downwards to the uplifted
left foot. This foot signifies release from bondage which is
the salvation of the devotee. The hand pointing towards it
is in the *gaja-hasta mudra,* like the outstretched trunk of
the elephant.

The whirl of dance movements also create a circle of
fire round him, *Prabha-mandala.* It signifies the vital
processes of the universe. This is the fire which at the end
of a *kalpa* destroys all. The drum heralds creation. The twin
functions of Creation and Destruction go side by side, as
without creation there can be no destruction and without
destruction, there can be no creation.

His aspect as *Vayu,* air is depicted by his flying garments
and *jata,* which dance and move when He dances. The stage
for His dance is His sky-form, Ether. The earth trembles
under His foot, waves arise, *Agni* flares up. The Whirlwind
is likened to his dance and the dust created are the ashes

with which Shiva's body is smeared. These ashes are formed
from the destruction of the universe and as the dance
proceeds, the ashes get scattered all around, forming a
pattern. The lines of the pattern are the lines of a plan for
the re-creation of the universe.

Shiva Nataraja wears a diadem, the crescent moon which
arose from the ocean of milk when it was churned for *amrita*,
the drink of immortality. Shiva as *Bhishaktanamurti* is the
Lord of Physicians, and the moon is the cup that holds the
ambrosia. Since Shiva wears the moon on his diadem, he
possesses the same qualities as the moon.

Shiva carries an image of Ganga, the personified river
Ganges, in his long tresses. He brought the celestial river
Ganga to water the parched earth and also so that the
shraddha for the ancestors of Bhagiratha could be performed.
The image of Ganga in his tresses represents Him in his
liquid form, the *Jalamayamurti.*

Nataraja is adorned with a garland of skulls. These skulls
belong to the Brahma's of previous aeons. The skulls laugh
at those who consider themselves immortal, a reminder to
all those who are born that they must die one day. Shiva
carries a sword which destroys the fear from which arises
misery. This sword in a sword of knowledge and cuts the
ignorance of mankind.

On his forehead, Shiva carries the *tripundra* mark. This
is made with the sacred ashes smeared with three fingers
along the forehead. It symbolises *trisatya,* the three forms
of truth in thought, word and deed. The marks also signify
the conquest of the three worlds by penance and austerity.
Similarly, the three strands of the sacred thread symbolise
the glory of the three *yugas.*

The dance of Shiva is an act of Creation. It arouses
dormant energies. These energies consist of five activities
of Shiva called *panchkriya,* i.e. *Srishti* (creation); *Stihthi*
(maintenance); *Samhara* (destruction); *Tiro-bhava* (re-
absorption, veiling or concealment, aloofness, display of *Maya
and Anugraha* (Favour, acceptance of the devotee). These
energies when gathered and projected into the evermoving
forces, form the energies of creation, preservation of forms
created and the ultimate destruction of the universe. This

is again followed by evolution, maintenance and destruction. This productive energy of the Absolute in its pristine strength represents the forces of evolution and involution, the appearance and disappearance of the universe. Shiva in this form is *Nritakari,* one who keeps the world rhythm going.

Though a destroyer, Shiva is kind-hearted. He destroyed *Kama* (love,lust) and came to be known as *Kamantaka,* and *Kala* (Time) and became *Kalantaka* but he continuously rejuvenates both of them. *Kama* is kept alive by the light emitting from the moon on his diadem which affects lovers, and he also creates a time factor assuring the eternal march of Time. By pulling aside the veil *(maya)* of darkness, he lets the light spread.

Every aspect of life has two opposing entities. *Deva* is the divine principle and *Bhuta* is matter. *Deva* is light, truth and immortality; *Bhuta* is darkness, untruth and death. One is positive and the other is negative; one is life, the other is inertia. The cycle of life and death can only proceed when these two basic opposite forces of good and evil, represented by the *Deva*s and the *Bhuta*s are finally reconciled. These two opposite priciples are eternally in conflict *(Daivasuram)* but become reconciled in the body of Shiva. Their co-existence is expressed in the rhythm of Shiva's dance.

Shiva's dance is the most inspiring and pragmatic act typifying the eternal rhythm which is the cause of the infinite creative process. He is the presiding deity of the mind. The entire universe created by Shiva is his Shakti or energy. It is like an ocean which fills all space and Shiva dances in the centre of this energy. His dance movements represent the movement of his *Shakti* or energy.

The dance of Shiva is compared to the rhythmic movements of the sun. The rhythm underlying both these movements is the basis of creation. Just as each of the solar systems has regular movements arranged round a fixed centre or axis, similarly Shiva dances inside a circle of fire flames. Sun in this context is not the physical body orb called the Sun but the visible form of the Supreme Soul or reality called Brahman. Brahman is compared to the lustre and radiation of the sun which brightens the four corners of space by its rays and also warms up the four directions of space.

Shiva is the auspicious one and in that respect he Creates, but as Rudra, he destroys. Shiva with his arms spread in dancing is described as a forest; His *jata* whirling during the dance, scatters flowers. Shiva's *jatabhara* contains the skull, symbol of death, as well as the crescent moon, symbol of growth and eternity. Presence of Ganga in his tresses, symbolise the elixir of life and sustenance, and the snake a symbol of transmigration of the eternal soul by the sloughing off of the snake skin.

Shiva as *Bhutapati* represents the five elements, the earth, water, fire, air and the sky, and his dance brings together in movement, all the essential charm in these five elements, i.e. the reflection in the gems, waves and ripples in the water, flames in the fire, movement in the wind, and the play of lightning.

Shiva is also depicted as embodying eternity as he overcomes Death itself. In Kalantaka, the dance of Time and Eternity, Shiva reveals himself as the Absolute and overcomes Death itself. As such, he is shown kicking Yama, the Lord of Death, with his left foot.

Shiva is a *Maha-yogi*. As Nataraja, the dreaded snake adorns his head along with the cool-rayed moon. Snake emits deadly poison and the moon offers *amrita*. Inspite of all forms of living creatures flocking to him, Shiva dances in the cremation grounds with the devastating fire in his forehead represented by his third eye and at the same time, he has the cool and refreshing waters of Ganga flowing on his crest. He is *Ishvara* and prosperity is assured only through his grace, yet he assumes the guise of a beggar, *(Bhikshantana murti)*. He is Hara who removes the bonds of cycles of birth and death. Sun is the visible form of Rudra-Shiva or the *Jyotir-linga*. His radiations are the rhythmic movements of Shiva's dance and the *linga* typifies the incomprehensible Supreme reality beyond Time and Space.

***

BIBLIOGRAPHY

AGARWALA, V.S.: Ancient Indian Folk Cults; Indian Civilization Series No. VII, Varanasi, 1970

————: Shiva Mahadeva; Veda Academy, Varanasi, 1965

————: Matsya-Purana, a study; All-India Kasiraj Trust, Varanasi, 1963

————: The Glorification of the Great Goddess; All-India Kasiraj Trust, Varanasi, 1963

————: Asiatic mythology, George G. Harrap & Co. London

BHATTACHARYYA, H.: Cultural Heritage of India

BHATTACHARYYA R.: Journal of the Oriental Institute, M.S. University of Baroda, Baroda, Sept.-Dec. Issue, Vol. XXII, 1972

CHAKROBORTI, H.: Pasupata-Sutram, Academic Publishers, Calcutta, 1970

COOMARASWAMY, A.: The Dance of Shiva; Asia Publishing House, Bombay, 1952

DANIELOU, A.: Hindu Polytheism; Routledge & Kegan Paul, London,1964

DUTT, M.N.: Garuda-Purana; Society for Resuscitation of Indian Literature, Calcutta, 1938

DUBOIS, J.A.: Hindu Manners, Customs and Ceremonies; Clarendon Press, Oxford, 1906

BANG, O.P.: "Concept of Smallpox Goddess in Part of W. Bengal", Men in India, Quarterly Journal, Jan-March Issue, 1973

FERGUSSON: Tree and Serpent Worship, London, 1920

GUBERNATIS, A.D.: Zoological Mythology, London, 1872

GUPTA, S.S.: Tree Symbol Worship in India; Indian Folklore Society, Bombay, 1965

GYANI, S.D.: Agni-Purana, a Study; The Chowkhamba Sanskrit Studies, Vol. XLII, Varanasi, 1964

HOPKINS, E.W.: The Religions of India, Edward Arnold, London, 1896

KRAMRISCH, S.: The Presence of Sivà; Oxford University Press, Delhi, 1981.

JAMES, E.O.: The Cult of the Mother Goddess, London, 1959

KEITH, A.B.: Religion and Philosophy of the Vedas; Harvard Oriental Series, Vol. 31, Harvard University Press, London, 1925

LONG, I.B.: "Festival of Repentance, a Study of Maha-Sivaratri," Journal of the Oriental Institute, M.S. University of Baroda, Baroda, Sept.-Dec. 1972, Vol.XXII

MAITY, P.K.: Historical Studies in the Cult of the Goddess Manasa, Punthi Pustak, Calcutta, 1896

OLDHAM, C.F.: The Sun and the Serpent, London, 1905

PERGITER, F.E.: The Markandeya-Purana; Indological Book House, Varanasi, 1969

RUKMANI, RAJAMANI: A Critical Study of the Bhagavata-Purana; The Chowkhambha Sanskrit Studies, Vol. LXXVII, 1970

SHASTRI, M.N.: Agni-Puranam; Chowkhambha Sanskrit Series Publication, Varanasi, 1967

SINHA & BASU: The History of Prostitution in India.

SHIVA-PURANA: Ancient Indian Tradition and Mythology series, Motilal Banarasidass, Delhi, 1970

SMITH, V.A.: History of Fine Arts in India and Ceylon

SWAMI SIVANANDA: Hindu Fasts & Festivals and their Philosophy; Yoga-Vedanta Forest Academy, Rishi-Kesh; 1962

THOMAS, P.: Epics, Myths and Legends of India; Taraporevala Sons & Co. Bombay, 1961

VOGEL, J. PH.: Indian Serpent Lore, London, 1926

VED KUMARI: The Nilamata-Purana, Vol.I; J & K Academy of Art, Culture & Language, Srinagar, 1968

WAVE, C.S.: Serpent Worship and Other Essays, London, 1885

WILSON, H.H.: Vishnu-Purana: Punthi Pustak, Calcutta, 1961

ZIMMER, H.: Myths & Symbols in Indian Art, Bollingen Series VI, Pantheon Books, USA., 1953

GLOSSARY

SHIVA

Adi	: a son of Andhakasura.
Aditi	: mother of gods; infinity, the boundless and endless heavens.
Adityas	: Solar divinities, 8 in number
Abhayahasta	: hand gesture showing fear not, a sign of protection
Aghora	: 4-faced form of Shiva, facing south, black in colour, holds an axe, shield, elephant hook, noose, spear, skull.
Agni	: God of Fire.
Agastya	: a mythical rishi mentioned in Rig-Veda.
Ahirbudhnya	: Rudra in his primeaval darkness.
Airavata	: Indra's elephant mount.
Aja	: a goat, the unborn, universal principle.
Aja-Ekapad	: Aja means unborn, Ekapad is one-footed, mainly an epithet of Rudra, though Brahma and Vishnu are also referred to as such.
Amba, Ambika, Ambalika	: three mothers mainly known as forms of Durga.
Ananta	: endless, boundless, eternal, infinite, the celestial serpent.
Aniruddha	: grandson of Krishna.
Andhaka	: son of Shiva and Parvati, born blind.
Aparna	: Parvati
Aparjita	: a 3-eyed goddess riding a lion, carries Shiva's emblems, unconquerable.
Apsara/s	: celestial dancers.
Apasmara purush	: demon of forgetfulness and lack of wisdom, lies prostrate at Shiva's feet.
Arjuna	: the third Pandava prince.

Ardh	:	means half.
Arundhati	:	wife of rishi Vasishtha.
Anugrahamurti	:	Shiva in his beneficent aspect.
Ardhanarishvara	:	Lord who is half man and half woman
Ashwins	:	the celestial physicians, twins born to the Sun-God.
Ashtamurti	:	eight-form murti of Shiva.
Asura/s	:	anti-gods of pre-vedic age; sons of Diti and Kashyapa.
Ashani	:	Akashmurti aspect of Shiva.
AUM	:	collectively Brahma, Vishnu, Shiva.
Ayyappen	:	Same as Shasta.
Badava mukha	:	a flame issuing from the ocean.
Baharupa	:	Tvashtr, the father of Visvarupa.
Balarama	:	elder brother of Krishna.
Bali	:	son of Virochana, grandson of Prahlada.
Bana, Banasura	:	ruler of Tezpur, Assam, devotee of Shiva, father of Usha.
Bana-lingas	:	lingas appeared on their own and not man made.
Bhaga	:	means the sharer.
Bhaganetra	:	an epithet of Shiva.
Bhagavata	:	dedicated to the service of god by singing his praise.
Bhadrakali	:	Durga.
Bhaktavatsala	:	Shiva favourably disposed towards his devotees.
Bhagiratha	:	a king who by his asceticism brought Ganga to earth.
Bhava	:	Rudra in his beneficent aspect.
Bhairava	:	most destructive aspect of Rudra.
Bhadra	:	wife of Brihaspati.
Bhauma	:	son of mother Earth.
Bhasma	:	ashes.
Bhima	:	Akashmurti of Shiva.
Bhishaktanamurti	:	Lord of all Physicians.
Bhringi	:	a sage, devotee of Shiva, refused to worship Parvati.

Bhuta	:	all demonic beings born of Shiva's anger, represent darkness, death. Earlier were considered as the elements.
Bhuta-ganas	:	troops of demons and goblins forming Shiva's army.
Bhutapati	:	The Lord of the elements:earth, water, fire, air, sky.
Bhumi	:	Earth personified.
Bhutesha, Bhuteshvara	:	an epithet of Shiva as the Lord of the elements.
Brahma	:	God of Creation, first of the Hindu triad of gods.
Brahmana	:	Priestly caste of Hindus.
Brahman	:	Impersonal, Supreme Soul.
Brahmasiras	:	the spear of Shiva, kills evil.
Brahmani	:	(i) a Shakti; (ii) a mind-born mother.
Brihaspati	:	a rishi with wide creative powers.
Bhasmasura	:	a demon killed by a ruse.
Bhrigu	:	a Vedic sage, one of the Prajapatis.
Chandravati	:	built a temple over the Jyotirlinga at Mallikarjuna.
Chamunda	:	Durga for having killed Chanda and Munda asuras.
Chandika	:	Durga, a name of Yoga Maya.
Chandrashekhara	:	Shiva having the moon in his hair.
Chitralekha	:	a portrait artist friend of Usha, daughter of Banasura.
Chanda	:	an asura killed by Durga
Damarukar, Damaru	:	drum, an emblem of Shiva.
Danava/s	:	a class of demons, sons of Danu and Diti.
Daitya/s	:	sons of Diti and Kashyapa
Daksha	:	father of Sati.
Devata/s	:	celestial beings.
Devasena	:	personified army of Indra, wife of Skanda.
Dhanwantri	:	Physician of gods.

Dhanya	:	mother of Sita.
Dharama	:	discipline righteousness, kindness an epithet of Yama who ministers justice to the dead.
Dharani	:	Mother Earth
Dhruva	:	fixed or immovable.
Dhurta	:	Skanda.
Dushana	:	a demon killed by Shiva at Mahakala Jyotirlinga.
Diksha	:	wife of Ugra.
Disha	:	wife of Bhima.
Diti	:	mother of Maruts, wife of Kashyapa.
Draupada	:	father of Draupadi.
Draupadi	:	wife of the five Pandava princes.
Durga	:	wife of Shiva.
Duryodhana	:	minister of Andhaka.
Dvapara-yuga	:	The 3rd era in Hindu mythology when Dharama possesses only two of the four legs of stability.
Dvarapala	:	gate keeper.
Ekaparna	:	Sister of Parvati.
Ekapatala	:	” ” ”
Gajahasta	:	elephant pose.
Gajanana	:	Ganesha, the elephant-faced god.
Gajasamhar	:	Shiva for killing a demon who attacked him in the form of an elephant.
Gana/s	:	Shiva's attendants, ghosts, ghouls, spirits.
Ganapati	:	Ganesha, the Lord of the Ganas.
Ganga	:	a sacred river, personified as a wife of Shiva.
Ganesha	:	the God with an elephant head.
Gangadhar	:	Shiva for receiving Ganga on his head.
Gandharava/s	:	celestial musicians.
Garuda	:	half-man, half-eagle mount of Vishnu.

Ghasmara	:	emissary of Jalandhar sent to Indra.
Ghora	:	Gana with a frightening face.
Gila	:	a general of Andhaka's army.
Girish	:	Shiva, the Lord of the mountains.
Girija	:	Parvati, the wife of Girish i.e Shiva.
Guha	:	Skanda.
Gunavati	:	female energy of Shiva as Ishvara.
Hara	:	Shiva as the Destroyer.
Hari-Hara	:	a combined murti of Vishnu and Shiva.
Harshana	:	an arrow of Kamadeva.
Himavat	:	personified Himalayas, father of Parvati.
Hiranyakasipu	:	brother of Hiranyaksha, father of Prahlada.
Hiranyaksha	:	a childless asura, adopted Andhaka.
Indra	:	God of rain and thunder.
Indrani	:	wife of Indra.
Ishana	:	Shiva's face looking upwards.
Ishvara	:	Shiva, the Supreme God, Surya-murti.
Jalamurti	:	Shiva in his liquid form represented by Ganga in his tresses.
Jalandhara	:	an evil being, married to Vrinda.
Janaka	:	father of Sita (epic Ramayana).
Jatadhara	:	having matted hair an epithet of Shiva.
Jaya	:	(i) Parvati; (ii) an attendant of Vishnu.
Jayanti	:	Parvati.
Jayant	:	Rudra representing the powers of Indra.
Jvarasura	:	the fever demon.
Jyoti-linga	:	not man made linga, arose on its own.

Kali	:	a form of Parvati, dark-complexioned; a name of a snake.
Kaliyuga	:	the last of the four yugas in Hindu mythology symbolising end of goodness.
Kalanemi	:	son of Virochana, father of Vrinda.
Kalp, Kalptaru	:	wish-fulfilling tree.
Kalantaka	:	Shiva overcomes death ,depicted as kicking Yama, the Lord of death.
Kalasamhara	:	destroyer of Time.
Kalavati	:	wife of Vrishabhana, mother of Radha.
Kamantakamurti	:	Shiva killing Kamadeva.
Kamadeva	:	God of love.
Kamandalu	:	ascetic's water pot.
Kamakhya	:	one of the Shakti-pithas.
Kamalaksha	:	son of Taraka asura.
Kamadhenu	:	wish-fulfilling cow.
Kapila	:	a sage, destroyed 60,000 sons of King Sagara.
Kapalin, Kapalamalin	:	Shiva wearing a garland of skülls.
Karttikeya	:	Skanda.
Kashyapa	:	a Vedic sage, one of the Sapta-rishis, married Diti.
Khatvanga	:	Shiva's club topped with a skull.
Khandesvara	:	Linga installed at Kashi.
Keshin	:	one with matted hair.
Kimpurush	:	an attendant of Kubera.
Kinnara/s	:	half-man, half-musicians at Kubera's palace.
Kirtimukha	:	a lion-headed monster, produced by Shiva, survived self-destruction even after eating his body except the head.
Kritya	:	a demoness, a terrible form, manifestation of Shiva.
Krishna	:	the eighth incarnation of Vishnu, embodiment of love.
Krittikas	:	6 discarded wives of rishis who nursed Skanda.

Krittivasa	:	Shiva, as the wearer of hides.
Kshatriyas	:	2nd of the four castes of Hindus, traditionally rulers and warriors.
Kshema	:	child of Ganesa and Siddhi.
Kubera	:	Lord of wealth.
Kumara	:	Skanda, the bachelor.
Kundalini	:	metabolic energy conceived as the serpent power in the human body.
Lakshmana	:	younger brother of Ramachandra.
Lakshmi	:	wife of Vishnu, goddess of beauty and prosperity.
Linga, Lingam	:	Shiva in his phallic form.
Lokapalas	:	guardians of the quarters, 4-8 in number.
Mahadeva	:	Shiva, the Great Lord.
Mahadevi	:	Parvati.
Mahashivaratri	:	The great festival of Shiva.
Maheshamurti	:	Shiva, the Great Lord.
Mahisha	:	an asura who attacked Durga and was killed by her.
Mandakini	:	a tributary of Ganga.
Manasa	:	the snake goddess, daughter of Shiva.
Mantra/s	:	hymns.
Maya	:	the architect of asuras.
Marichi	:	uncle of Ravana.
Maruts	:	gods of wind, sons of Diti and Kashyapa.
Martand	:	Surya, son of Aditi.
Mayamoha	:	a delusive teacher created by Vishnu.
Mena	:	mother of Parvati.
Modakas	:	sacrificial sweet cakes.
Mohini	:	Vishnu as a beautiful, seductive woman.
Moksha	:	salvation.
Mohana	:	arrow of Kamadeva.

Mrigashiras	:	head of a deer cut off from the body, remains in the sky.
Mrityumjaya	:	Shiva, the death conquering deity.
Murti	:	an icon.
Mula prakriti	:	Parvati.
Munda	:	an asura killed by Durga
Naag	:	serpent.
Nairrata	:	imp, goblin, rakshasa.
Nairriti	:	female energy of Nairrata.
Nandi	:	a bull, Shiva's mount.
Nandikeshvara	:	Shiva, the Lord of Nandi.
Narada	:	a rishi.
Narasimha	:	(Nrsimha) half-man, half-lion incarnation of Vishnu.
Narayani	:	female energy of Narayana.
Nartakari	:	Shiva, the Lord of dance, who keeps the world rhythm going.
Nataraja	:	Shiva, the Lord of dance.
Navagrahas	:	nine planets of Hindu astronomy.
Nilakantha	:	Shiva with a blue throat.
Nisumbha	:	a general of Jalandhra's army.
Nritamurti	:	Shiva, Lord of dancers.
Panchanana	:	5-faced image of Shiva.
Parjanya	:	Indra, the Lord of rain.
Parashu	:	axe.
Parashurama	:	a part incarnation of Vishnu.
Parvati	:	wife of Shiva.
Pasha	:	bondage.
Pashu	:	ego, as well as animals.
Pashupati	:	Shiva, the protector of animals and souls.
Pasupata	:	spear of Shiva, kills evil.
Patala	:	netherworld.
Pati	:	Lord.
Pinaki, Pinakin.	:	Rudra-Shiva wielding the bow Pinakin, signifies the destructive powers of Shiva.

Pinaka	:	bow of Shiva.
Pishachas	:	evil spirits.
Pradyumna	:	son of Krishna, father of Aniruddha.
Pradhana	:	chief.
Prajapati	:	Brahma.
Prahlada	:	son of Hiranyakasipu.
Prakriti	:	the original form, the source of all that is and all that is to come.
Pramathas	:	Shiva's ganas, deformed beings.
Prithu	:	the first king, started agriculture, considered a minor incarnation of Vishnu.
Puranas	:	ancient texts.
Pushan	:	a vedic deity, identified with the Sun.
Purush	:	The Supreme Being as the original eternal man, identified with Brahma, Vishnu and Shiva.
Rahu	:	a daitya, son of Vipracitti and Simhika; ascending node in Hindu astronomy, causes eclipses by periodically swallowing the moon and the sun.
Raivata	:	presiding constellation of animals, signifies nourishment and immortality.
Rajas	:	passion.
Rakshasas	:	evil beings.
Raktavati	:	maid of Shitala, has power over measles.
Ramachandra	:	7th incarnation of Vishnu, eldest son of Dashratha of the Solar dynasty.
Rati	:	desire personified, wife of Kamadeva.
Ravana	:	evil king of Lanka, abducted Sita, killed by Ramachandar
Ravananugrahamurti	:	Shiva having compassion on Ravana.
Rishi/s	:	holy men, authors, and singers of Vedic hymns.

Rohini	:	foster mother of Balarama.
Rudra	:	Vedic name of Shiva.
Rudragana	:	ganas of Rudra.
Rudraksha	:	a rosary made of the beads of Eleocarpus Sphaericus.
Sadashiva	:	Shiva of pure nature possessed 3 energies: Saraswati, Lakshmi, Parvati, wives of Brahma, Vishnu, Shiva respectively, considered as different manifestations of Shiva.
Sadyojata	:	Skanda, the violent hero, also an epithet of Shiva.
Samhara	:	destruction, involution.
Samharamurti	:	destructive aspect of Shiva.
Sanaka	:	mind-born son of Shiva.
Sananata Kumara	:	mind born son of Shiva.
Sandhya	:	twilight personified as Brahma's daughter; wife of Shiva.
Sanjivini-vidya	:	knowledge of bringing dead, alive.
Saptarishi/s	:	7 great rishis, their names vary in different accounts.
Sarga	:	son of Bhima and Disha.
Sarva	:	a Vedic deity of destruction, later associated with Shiva.
Sarvamangala	:	Parvati, Ambika.
Saraswati	:	a Vedic goddess of wisdom, speech, art, music, learning.
Sati	:	daughter of Daksha, wife of Shiva.
Sattva	:	truth, purity, cohesion.
Savitra	:	Rudra as well as Surya, source of heat and light respectively.
Senani	:	Skanda, the chief of the army.
Siddhas	:	semi-divine beings living in the region between the earth and the sun, realised souls.
Siddhi	:	wife of Ganesha.
Siva-linga	:	the phallic emblem of Shiva.
Shaiva, Shaivite	:	devotee of Shiva.
Shakti	:	female power of gods.

Shaktidhara	:	Skanda, for carrying a spear called Shakti.
Shakti-pitha/s	:	places of pilgrimage where pieces of Sati fell after her death.
Shamshanvasi	:	one who resides in the cremation grounds.
Shankara	:	Shiva, the auspicious God, source of boundless joy.
Shantanu	:	husband of Ganga in the Mahabharata.
Shasta	:	son of Shiva and Vishnu in his female form of Mohini.
Sharabha	:	a mythical animal form of Shiva with 8 feet, part animal and part bird.
Shesha	:	(the remainder) a divine snake.
Shiva	:	wife of Ishana, son Manojna.
Shiva	:	a male form, a God who destroys evil, the third of the Hindu triad of gods.
Shivaratri	:	festival of Shiva.
Shitala	:	goddess of smallpox.
Shraddha	:	ceremony performed for the ancestors
Shumbha	:	a general of Jalandhara's army.
Shukra	:	priest of the asuras
Shyama	:	dark-complexioned.
Skanda	:	son of Shiva and Parvati.
Soma	:	moon deified.
Soma-Skanda	:	Skanda in the company of his parents.
Srishti	:	creation-evolution.
Sthiti	:	preservation.
Sthanu	:	Immovable, immutable.
Sudarshana chakra	:	Vishnu's discus.
Surya	:	the Sun god.
Sunda	:	a daitya.
Svaha	:	wife of Prajapati
Svadha	:	daughter of Daksha, mother of Mena, Dhanya, Kalavati.

Tamas	:	quality of darkness, disintegration.
Taraka, Tarakasura		: an asura killed by Skanda.
Tarakaksha	:	son of Tarakasura.
Tat-purusha	:	Shiva's head facing east, represents the Supreme man.
Tillotma	:	a celestial damsel.
Tirobhava	:	deluding, veiling.
Tri-aksha	:	Shiva, the 3-eyed.
Triambaka	:	” ” ”
Tri-nayana	:	” ” ”
Trinetra	:	” ” ”
Tripura-Sundari	:	Parvati, the most beautiful woman in the three worlds.
Tripuras	:	residents of the three cities.
Tripurari, Tripuntkara	: Shiva, the destroyer of Tripuras.
Tripundra	:	a shaivite sign of 3-horizontal lines on the forehead.
Trisatya	:	the three truths symbolised by tripundra are, truth in thought, word and deed.
Tvashter	:	fashions different types of living creatures.
Ucchaishiravas	:	celestial horse of Indra
Ugra	:	Tatpurusha, Vayu murti of Shiva.
Ugra-Kumara	:	Skanda, the violent hero.
Uma	:	same as Parvati, wife of Shiva.
Uma-Maheshvara	:	Shiva, husband of Uma.
Upasunda	:	a daitya.
Upavita	:	sacred thread.
Utpala	:	asura destroyed by Parvati's ball.
Vaidhasa	:	minister of Andhaka.
Vaidyanatha	:	Lord of Physicians.
Vaivasvata	:	son of Surya.
Vaishnava	:	devotee of Vishnu.
Vamadeva	:	Shiva's head facing west, red in colour, left-handed.
Varuna	:	Vedic deity, Lord of Ocean.
Varuni	:	Goddess of Wine, wife of Varuna.

Varaha	:	Boar incarnation of Vishnu.
Vasu	:	8 deities, personification of natural phenomena.
Vasant, Vasanta	:	spring season, epithet of Shitala.
Vasishtha	:	a rishi.
Veda/s	:	sacred books of Hindus.
Vedic	:	pertaining to the Vedas.
Vetala/s	:	vampires who animate dead bodies, haunt cremation grounds, one of Shiva's attendants.
Vidala	:	asura destroyed by Parvati's ball.
Vidunmali	:	son of Tarakasura.
Vighnasura	:	demon of destruction.
Vighnaraja	:	Ganesha whom Vighnasura accepted as a lord.
Vighneshwara	:	Ganesha for removing obstacles.
Vighasa	:	a daitya messenger of Andhaka.
Vijaya	:	Parvati.
Virabhadra	:	a demon created by Shiva to destroy Daksha's Yajna.
Viraka	:	Skanda.
Virshabha, Virsha	:	Nandi, the vehicle of Shiva.
Virupaksha	:	Shiva for possessing three eyes.
Virata	:	a king, devotee of Shiva.
Vishnu	:	the second god of the Hindu trinity of gods.
Vishwanatha	:	Lord of the universe.
Vishwarupa	:	all pervading Vishnu.
Vishwakarman	:	the celestial architect.
Vrinda	:	wife of Jalandhar.
Vyas	:	compiler of the Mahabharata.
Yaksha/s	:	tree and water nymphs.
Yajna	:	sacrifice.
Yama	:	Lord of death.
Yamya	:	female energy of Yama.
Yoga	:	discipline of mind and body.
Yogamaya	:	Vishnu's sister, married Shiva.
Yogeshvara	:	Shiva as the arch-yogi.

INDEX

Abhinandana : 37
Adi: 75
Aditi: 21, 22, 24
Aditya : 43, 52, 86
Agastya : 100
Aghora : 2, 6, 46
Agni : 4, 6, 15, 16, 28, 30-33, 35,
    43, 53, 55, 67, 72, 99, 103,
    104, 107, 120
Agni-murti : 6
Ahirbudhnya : 43
Ahi-Vritra : 43
Airavata : 35, 62, 66, 72, 104
Aja : 24, 43
Aja-Ekapad : 43
Akasha, Akasha-Murti : 6, 14
Alakshmi : 16
Amba : 29, 44, 73, 77
Ambika : 8, 29, 44, 73, 105, 107-
    109, 111
Ambalika : 8, 44, 73
Ananta : 53
Andhaka, Andhakasura : 75-79,
    80-84, 86.
Aniruddha : 58-60

Annapurna : 18
Apana : 6
Aparna : 26
Aparjita : 44
Apasmara Purush: 119
Arhat : 49
Ardhanareshvara: 2, 98, 99
Arjuna : 10, 96, 97
Arundhati : 32
Anugrahamurti: 1, 46, 121
Arunaksha : 115
Ashwins : 43
Ashani : 5, 6, 7
Ashtamurti : 2, 3, 6
Asi-loman : 105
Asura/s : 3, 15, 20, 30, 34, 46-
    52, 54-56, 58-65, 68, 69,
    77, 84, 95, 103, 105, 106,
    108-117.
Ayyapen : 95

Badava-Mukha : 30
Balagraha : 35
Balarama : 59, 60
Bali : 62

ILLUSTRATIONS

1. Ekamukha Shiva-linga from Khoh, Allahabad Museum,
c. 6th cent. A.D.

2. Pashupati, a seal from Mohenjodaro, c. 2500 B.C.

3. Shiva as Aghora; Iraveteshwar Darasuram Temple,
c. 11th cent. A.D.

4. Shiva as Bhikshatanamurti, Tanjore.

5. Rudra and Bhikshadanan murti of Shiva, Madurai,
Tamil Nadu, 17th cent. A.D.

6. Shiva as Ishan, Khiching, Orissa, c. 10th-11th cent. A.D.

7. Shiva as Nilakantha, Brihadeshwar Temple, Tanjore,
c. 11th cent. A.D.

8. Shiva Gajasamharamurti, Madurai, c. 17th cent. A.D.

9. Shiva, Parashvanath Temple, Khajuraho, 9th-10th cent. A.D.

10. Ashtamurti of Shiva, Parel, Bombay.

11. Shiva as Martanda-Bhairava, Darasuram, c. 12th cent. A.D.

12. Trimurti of Shiva, Elephanta Caves, Bombay, 6th cent. A.D.

13. Sadashiva, Indian Museum, Calcutta, 11th 12th cent. A.D.

14. Nandi, the Mount of Shiva, Chamunda Hills, Mysore
13th cent. A.D.

15. Madana (Kamadeva), the god of love, accompanied by his wife Rati; Chinnakeshava Temple, Belur, 12th-13th cent. A.D.

16. Shiva Kamantakamurti, Darasuram. c. 12th cent. A.D.

17. Marriage of Shiva and Parvati, Ellora, Cave No. 29, 6th cent. A.D.

18. Bronze bust of Parvati as Tripura-Sundari, Tanjore Art
Gallery, 12th-13th cent. A.D.

19. Parvati, the beautiful daughter of the mountains, Indian Museum,
Calcutta, 11th-12th cent. A.D.

20. Shiva with his consort, Parvati, popularly called Uma-
Maheshwara, Indian Museum, Calcutta,
9th-10th cent. A.D.

21. Parvati, the compassionate one (Karunthalankudi) Tanjore.

22. Dancing Ganesha from Kanauj, Lucknow Museum, c. 8th-
9th cent. A.D.

23. Head of Parvati, Ahichchatra, 5th cent. A.D.

24. Arjuna approaching Shiva, Shiva-keshava Temple, Pushpagiri, Cuddapah.

25. Ganga, the wife of Shiva, Bihar, 8th cent. A.D.

26. Preta, companion of Shiva, Lingaraja Temple, Bhubaneshwar, 11th cent. A.D.

27. Shiva Bhairava, Ekapada Someshwara Temple, Mukhalingam,
10th-11th cent. A.D.

28. Shani, Rahu and Ketu, Navagraha Slab, Konarak, 13th cent. A.D.

29. Churning the Ocean of Milk, Mallikarjuna Temple, Pattadkal 7th cent. A.D., Karnataka.

30. Wives of the Sapta Rishis, Tanjore Gallery.

31. Shiva Somaskandamurti, Chidambaram,
c. 12th cent. A.D.

32. Karttikeya, Indian Museum, Calcutta, 11th-12th cent. A.D.

33.   Parashurama, Garhwa Fort, c. 9th cent. A.D.

34. Trimurti of Shiva, unprotected monument, Mukhalingam,

35. Ravana shaking the Kailash Mountain, Virupaksha Temple, Pattadkal, 7th cent. A.D.

36. Shiva carrying the corpse of Sati, bronze piece in the
Gwalior Museum.

37. Descent of the Ganges, Mahabalipuram, c. 700 A.D.

38. Gandharva and Apsara, the flying celestials, Badami,
7th cent. A.D.

39. Agni, the god of Fire, Mathura Museum, 8th cent. A.D.

40. A dwarf, a gana of Shiva, Allahabad Museum

41. Brahma, the Creator, Aihole, 7th cent. A.D.

42. Chaturmukha Linga, Indian Museum, Calcutta.

43. Shiva Ardhanarishvara, Gangaikondacholapuram,
c. 11th cent. A.D.

44. Durga ready to kill evil, from Bhitari in Lucknow Museum, 8th cent. A.D.

45. Sapta-matrikas from Nalanda, Lucknow Museum, c. 8th-9th cent. A.D.

46. Chamunda, Asutosh Museum, Calcutta, c. 10th cent. A.D.

47. Kali, the personification of death and destruction, a bronze sculpture, Gwalior Museum.

48. Durga as Mahishasuramardini from Abaneri, Rajasthan, 10th cent. A.D.

49. Dakshinamurti of Shiva, Tanjore Art Gallery.

50. Durga as Mahishasuramardhini from Abaneri, Rajasthan, 9th cent. A.D.

51. Shiva manifests himself in linga form, Brihadeshwar
Temple, Tanjore, c. 11th cent. A.D., Tamil Nadu.

52. Shiva worship, Ellora Cave No. 16, c. 6th-7th cent. A.D.

53.   Shiva from Gudimallan, 2nd cent. B.C.

54. Shiva Nataraja, Gangaikondacholapuram, 11th cent. A.D. Tamil Nadu.